Journey into life

Kamyar Hekmat MA, DDS

DEDICATION

I dedicate this book to my children Paulina and Kevin whose constant laughter and joy strengthened me in every step of my life

Acknowledgement

I acknowledge Shilla Hekmat for giving me the
opportunity to experience life as it presented itself to me.

ABOUT THE AUTHOR

Kamyar Hekmat has had years of experience interacting with many different people of different backgrounds. Based on his interactions and observations, he has compiled a set of experiences and lessons that have been introduced in his book Journey Into Life. His wish is for readers to become observant of the lives they lead and get an insight into creating a better life for themselves. He believes that each person is in essence good and with good intentions, and it is his/her experiences that shape what legacy is left behind.

PROLOGUE

Often, as we live our lives, we become so entangled in the daily chores of life that we forget to take a step aside and observe ourselves and see things either as they truly are or sometimes as something that could be seen differently with different meanings and consequences. It is my belief that our thought process or what thought we are having that day or moment, even from other people in our lives, affects how and what we think of the people we are facing and our view of what we are facing. There is a reason for everything that shows up in our lives and many times, we suffer because of our fears and allow our fears to guide the path that we travel. Sometimes, if we pay attention to what could or has otherwise evolved, we can train our thoughts to look at life more wisely. If we train ourselves to replace fear with love, we find that many times, the problems will disappear because two opposites cannot exist in the same place at the same time. There are many times when we can replay instances in our lives and do it differently, with more love and less fear, and find ourselves in a stronger place of happiness, satisfaction, and contentment. My hope and desire in putting this book together is to raise the awareness we need so that we can live fuller lives with more positive experiences and become our own coaches in creating a better vision of how to overcome obstacles and challenges and allow hope to give us a better way to experience our life.

TABLE OF CONTENTS

CHAPTER 1

I am being taken down the aisle in a beautiful tuxedo at a gathering, which I always imagined would be a not-so-joyful celebration. The mood around is somber. Somehow, I expected it to turn out more fun, but I was caught by surprise one more time. The unexpected has occurred again, and everyone around me is staring at me in disbelief again. But why? Isn't this the way it was written to be? I feel ecstatic. I have reached my goal, and I have lived a good life. I am proud of what I've been and what I've done. I see some eyes full of tears and some full of awe. Some eyes are staring into the deep blue sky, and some are stuck motionless, digging into the deepest thoughts. The only thought in my mind, though, is what will happen now that I can't change things. How will they move on? How will nature, events, or destiny lead my loved ones?

In the crowd, I see the two happy faces that I have cherished all my life. How comforting to see them feel my joy of the moment. Only they seem to realize that what was and what is has left them richer with love and strength. The passion that we brewed for each other through the years can only grow closer to perfection with the passing of every moment. Though it is believed that once the touch leaves, the mind has a way of fading the memories away, the destiny point of my life with the special mindful memories will always survive the test of time.

I will never forget that day when I was walking with my 4-year-old son to Souplantation for dinner when I told my son that I want him to be happy even when I'm not around, and he responded:" Dad, you will always be around because you are in my heart."

And that is how my Journey into Life started.

Chapter 2
Finally, Heaven is Here

It is the day after I was taken down the Isle. I remember vividly how crummy everything was before, and now, all of a sudden, I've opened a door, and on the other side, I see this beautiful scene. The smell of fresh, clean air, a beautiful sunrise, a gorgeously blue (my favorite color) sky, everything organized the way it should be. It is truly heaven. I cannot believe it, but it seems I'm there; the door is open to me, and all I have to do is step through this doorway, and a whole new life and experience awaits me. I look behind me, and all I see is peace and quietness as if everyone is still asleep. It appears early in the morning, and nobody has arrived yet. I tell myself to leave the door open so when the others arrive, they can see which way to go. A man arrives, Godly in nature, says his prayers, and follows through the open door. I walk through the door and leave the door open. I'm there. What a feeling of ecstasy. My whole body is relaxed. Because I left the door open, I know whenever someone I love wants to find me, they can. Now I'm happy I've left.

Now I know why I had to leave. I was so powerless back there; I could not convince people of what I thought was best. I could not make them happy nor myself happy. I could not add to anyone's life. I did what I did for the kids, and I got them where they are. I don't know if that is where they should be, but I know I've guided them down the right path in the right way, and now they have the power to take it on by themselves for the rest of the way. I know that they know I'm fine and happy. I want everybody else to know I'm well and happy.

Now, here, I don't see the need to change anybody or to change anything for anybody. Everything is the way it should be, and surprisingly, it is to my liking. That is what makes this trip worthwhile. Things are the way they should be; there is no more trial and error, no more unknowns. No more guesses, no more what to do's and how to do's. By the way, I hope you know this does not mean I have any regrets. I really don't. It's just that this is much better. Much, much better.

CHAPTER 3
LIFE UNEXPECTED
2/28/1999

And so another seemingly endless day comes to a close. When I opened my eyes this morning, I never expected to see, hear, or feel all the things that I did today. I thought it was going to be another routine day. I started to get my act together to let things go on the happy road. I called my sister because I knew she enjoyed seeing me. She got some words out of me and gave me some words of wisdom. I was looking forward to that. But then I never expected the rest of the things. But who said life has to be smooth and expected?

So, I spent my day going from one ailing person to another, although the two men were drastically different in age: my father-in-law, 60, and my son, 6. But when I was sitting on the rocking chair, the scene looked horridly similar to the scene I had seen earlier that morning at the house on top of the hills.

The two men were lying peacefully on their backs, letting the air in and out rapidly, with their eyes closed and their senses numb, almost communicating with each other through the heavenly medium. Again, I found myself sitting a few feet away from my son, worrying and praying for his health, wondering when God would give us the freedom to enjoy the life that was trusted with us. I could hear the music, the piano tunes from "Perchance to Dream," roaring in my mind, reminiscing the events of about six years ago. It struck me again because earlier today, I had thought of that day again while we were at the school carnival. I had bought a bunch of tickets for my kids and divided them equally so they could have the chance to play whatever they chose and go on any rides they wanted. I just stood afar and watched them run excitedly from one place to another. I was just getting flashbacks from the time when I couldn't have the luxury of doing that because of my fight with cancer.

At the carnival, my son ran out of ticket money while his sister had enough to go for a pony ride. I could see the strong desire in his eyes wishing for a miracle to land two more Dollar tickets in his T-shirt pocket so he could go on the pony ride with his sister. But no such miracle was about to happen because I had told them very seriously that when they ran out of play tickets, I would not buy them anymore. And I was not about to change my word. After all, I always thought I should be a man of principle, even though sometimes it should not matter and should be bypassed. Suddenly, he found enough power and courage to come up to me and ask for two more dollars for the tickets. And, of course, I clarified to him the bad news of no more. I saw him walk away in acceptance, but yet wishful and disappointed.

That was when the scene from when he was in the hospital six years ago appeared in front of my eyes, and I told myself that for all the injustice that was done to him, to rob him of those fun, happy days of infancy, to rob him of his beloved grandma when he was 4, can't I give something as easy and simple as a 2 dollar pony ride to him?

I became determined to eat my pride and swallow my words to give him that moment of joy because, again, I said, "I don't know what is going to happen tomorrow." I found a way to save face, so I offered to buy from him the silly rubber dinosaur that he had won in a silly previous game, conveniently for two dollars. Luckily, my offer was accepted, and off he ran with the two dollars with a big smile on his face. I loved seeing the look of triumph on his face. A moment to be treasured again was just carved in my mind for good. In a dash, he was on the pony with his sister, and I don't know anything better I could have done with that moment in my life.

CHAPTER 4
THE RETURN FROM PALM SPRINGS
APRIL 1999

I came back from a short vacation and was immediately put to the test of life. As if it wasn't enough to have experienced two of the biggest disasters in one's life (having a near-death experience with cancer and suddenly losing a parent) within a year's time on separate occasions, now I had to face the same disasters simultaneously even though I'm not the subject now. But it is still as hurtful. As much as I try to distance myself from it, the emotions, fears, and lack of trust in life come back to life in my memory.

But within all these experiences, I find that there is still more to it. I am in a matter of 10 minutes being consulted for preparation for the death of a loved one and the wedding of another loved one. It seems that in a matter of 2 weeks, there are going to be four ceremonies: 2 for celebrating one's life and memorializing him, and the other 2 for joining two hands together to start a new life and celebrate the beginning of a united life.

I can almost not feel my feelings. I cannot comprehend how to associate with these events. It seems to me as if going through it once was not enough; now I have to practice living the experience from the other side of the fence also, to experience the experience from a different angle as if The Almighty worried that I might forget the first set of lessons and tests that were delivered to me.

The only way I can describe the events from last Friday to this Sunday night is that I am being trained and prepared to experience the next level of life or maybe another life. Maybe these are the final touches to the portrait. The scenes from my life today have all been trying to give me a lesson and a different perspective on life. Earlier, I went to play tennis, and on the court next to mine, there were two handicapped players in wheelchairs who were skillfully playing tennis together. Then, while planning for a wedding and all the fun, I had to be reminded of the life and soul that was going to leave us. From the two tennis players on the wheelchairs that flabbergasted me to find out that all good things have bad moments associated with them, I learned that if I am not happy or satisfied, it is not that there is something wrong with others, but it is just the way life is. These have all given me a hint to carry with me so I can be more prepared to face the challenges of the next phase of life.

Again, what I'm happy and thankful for is that I have had a chance to give my love, support life, stories, and life lessons to my two wonderful kids. I know because of my experiences and my being, they are better equipped to face their lives in a happier fashion with greater peace and love for happiness and freedom. That is my happiness. I have achieved what was to be achieved for me personally.

CHAPTER 5
WHAT IS IN STORE TOMORROW
10/19/99

I attack each day with force and zeal, expecting to be something more than I was the day before. I keep my head above water and keep going against all odds, looking forward to the day that I will get to reap the rewards of my hard, honest work in life. Often, I ask myself, "Is there really a reward for all that I have done and tried to do in my life." Does it show anywhere? Is the reward "death"? Is timely moving on really the goal we are all trying to reach, and when we have reached it, that is success in life? Do those who die early reach the end successfully sooner than estimated? Therefore, having completed their mission, they are taken away to the next game. The next level. Is the next level going to get harder with more to achieve before success?

I don't know when the end is or is going to be. Last night, as I was looking through my picture album, I came across my mom's photo of 6/27/97. Her last photo with the kids. Her last dinner with us and the kids. She was happily sitting with the kids and exchanging gifts and the poems she had written for them. Did she know? Did she have any idea that that was going to be it? Would she have done anything differently had she known? Would we have done anything differently had we known? Does it matter in the whole arena of life? Would we have been living differently had we known? Are we living differently now that we know? Would we live differently if we knew this was our last day, week, month, or year? It has got to be such that when we are gone, there are no regrets, none whatsoever. No regrets from us for ourselves, and no regrets from others for us, and no regrets from others for themselves. Me, you, and they should know that we have lived life the way we would have even if we had known this is the last picture, the last dinner, the last day, the last word.

So now that I'm faced with my knee problem and pain that appears unknown, considering the history that I had with the cancerous tumor in my neck, I ask myself if this is how it is all going to end. Is this my lifespan? Have I done what I was meant to do in life? Am I satisfied with what I have done in life? I tell my son when they are playing soccer that you don't get a prize for running after the ball; you only get a prize if you finish by stealing or kicking the ball. End the pursuit. Hit the goal. Get a point.

Have I been running after the ball all my life without delivering the final punch? Am I or my mission complete? I don't think so; I think I'm at the halfway point of the race to my mission. But I have lost track of my mission. What am I supposed to do? What am I supposed to follow? I'm so lost. Does the end come when you are lost? Do you slide down to square one when you lose track of your mission or when you step out of your path so far that no hope for return is in sight? Have I stepped out of my path, or has life pushed me out of my path? Does it matter? Is the consequence any different? Do I get any points for the time that I was on track?

So many questions remain and continuously arise. I feel that as long as questions remain, there is work to be done. There are challenges to be met and overcome, goals to be reached, and actions to be taken. I still need to pursue my dream and not assume that I have been pushed off my track just because an immense challenge has been presented to me. Actually, maybe this challenge is trying to get me on the track to greatness. I need to accept the challenge of becoming the captain of my ship and guiding it to the shore.

CHAPTER 6
ANGER
11/11/1999

Everybody is angry. Everywhere I look, there is anger brewing. A fly zips by, and anger is in the air. An ant speaks, and anger bursts out. What is this anger that has so much power? How strong is it that it is everywhere, is being spent every minute, and it never ends? Where does this anger get its energy from? Why has it taken over our lives? Why is it stronger than happiness? Or is it? Can we get rid of this anger by forcing happiness into our lives, or can we bring happiness into our lives if we force anger out? Does anger bring happiness? Does it make us feel good? Certainly not. So why does it find a place in our hearts? Why do we carry it along with us?

I make a wish.

I wished all humanity would put away all anger. They would mean no harm and understand that no one else means harm. I wish that everyone would understand that all words said to come from the heart and are meant to bring peace and happiness to the family and community. Of course, my wish will not apply to governments and large populations. My wish is only meant to apply to families and close friends. To work between members of families. Can you see how much hurt this would take away if people would understand that the essence of all people is good? That if a brother or sister, or mother or father, or son or daughter says something, it is not to hurt anyone. It is not to cause anger. It is only an expression of their mood, feelings, and state of mind. It does not need any response. It does not need to be reciprocated. It does not need to be the beginning of a series of other heartfelt experiences. It rather means that that person needs something. It is their reaching out for help. And if one is reaching out for help with the demonstration of anger, you should not respond with anger. You should rather embrace and show Love, support, and affection. You should absorb anger and emit peace, show empathy, have compassion, and be curious.

You should reach the root of the anger that is embedded in the ground and not hold the tree responsible for the rotten fruit.

CHAPTER 7
I'M NOT ALONE.
6/1/2000

I've just come home from a Wellness Community session where I, as well as people like me, got to talk. It is a cancer survivor support group. Such a sense of euphoria has taken over me. Suddenly, I realize I'm not alone. I'm not strange. My feelings are not wrong. I am not a disaster. I'm not bad nor broken. I saw that a lot of other people who went through the same experience as me-dealing with the diagnosis of cancer and the subsequent chemotherapy- were experiencing the same things. The emotional ups and downs. How other people could not understand us. Life has changed so much for us, and it is okay that it has changed. We can accept and move on with the changes, but others cannot accept our changes and want to follow the old path. It was really helpful to get my feelings validated.

I had waited more than three years before I decided to go to this program. I suffered a lot needlessly. I should have started this sooner before it started to affect my personal relationships. What a relief it was to find out that I was not the only one fighting fatigue, and fatigue is not depression. I also found how some people got over their fatigue by naturotherapy and exercise therapy. I understood how others also feel like damaged goods at times and how it affects our relationship with others. Just because we felt we were a minority of the population afflicted with this condition, we were all feeling like an outcast. We had lost our self-confidence and self-worth. We thought that now that we have been blessed to survive, we should have no more desires and demands of life. I learned that I should not have any expectations of the future, but it is fine to have desires and visions of a fabulous future. The sense of friendship and support that we all got made each one of us stronger as the sessions continued. It is huge to suddenly see the path of life change and be forced to live a different way. It takes time for me to get used to and accept it, and it takes time for others to understand my process.

I feel relieved that others also share my struggle, which has led me to be tired and worried. I feel helpless, but so do many others. It is ok to need help and want help and get help, even if all my life, my pride didn't allow me to ask or get help. What is the quick way out? I don't know, but we will begin here with a new mindset, belief system, and action plan as the journey into life continues.

CHAPTER 8
SO, WHERE DO WE GO FROM HERE?
3/5/2001

Life hasn't been fair, and it never will be.

Life hasn't been just, and I wonder if it ever will be.

This is the life and experiences that I have to live with.

I cannot buy a new life, not with money nor with prayer.

Nobody is going to give me anything more.

I might have had to settle for a lot less than what I have now.

What I have now is pretty good.

I am not happy with what is there now, but that is my problem and not life's problem.

Even if God decided on this life for me, there is no word to judge this program.

I am the only person who can add to or change this program.

I am the only person who can change the perception of what this program is.

I am the only person who can change the expectations I had from this program.

I am the creator of the expectations that have led to pain and disappointment.

I am the only one who would benefit from the way I perceive this program because everybody else lives their own program.

I am the only one who can shift expectations and change the way the results and outcomes are seen, and I am the only one who can change the results.

Therefore, I will live this life the way I live it, with all of its good and bad.

I make the happenings.

CHAPTER 9
THE SOCCER EXPERIENCE
3/5/2001

Back in September, I started to coach AYSO soccer. The day I started, I was asking myself what I was doing here. I did not know a thing about coaching, but yet I was very excited. I was testing the water to see how good I am with kids. With motivating them, understanding them, guessing them, and leading them. After six months, 20 games, 15 wins, two ties, and three losses, I now know that I know kids. I'm good at guessing what they need, what helps them, and what is correct. My confidence in my judgment has increased tremendously. I'm good with knowing what they need to practice to get them where they want to be. I dedicated myself to what I was set to do, and I achieved more than I ever expected. I realized that whatever thought I planted in their heads, they would make it come to a realization. The thought, whether negative or positive, had so much power. One time, we were down 3-0 at halftime, and so at the break, I told them how in a European championship game, one team was down three goals at halftime, and they came back to win the game, and so guess what, my team did too. Children are so innocent, and their minds are such good creators. Therefore, one must only feed into it what one wants to see come true.

One other thing that I learned for sure is that the unexpected always wins over what is expected. When I started the soccer season, I never thought I would have so many wins. The kids on my team, except for one, were not such amazing players. But what I managed to do was to bring the best out in each of those kids, and I made each one of them feel that they contributed to the win equally, and that is how I got such a coherent group of players. I remember the players had developed such a sense of togetherness and commitment that one time, it was pouring rain, and more than half the team showed up for practice at the field. We all had so much fun playing soccer in the rain.

In life, it doesn't matter how good someone is; just making them feel that they are good makes them much more competent, especially when they feel they are part of a coherent group or community. Comradery, social belongingness, and mutual respect are what put a team in a winning position.

CHAPTER 10
LIFE BEHAVES IN THE MOST COMPLICATED MANNER.
6/12/2001

I have always believed that life desires simplicity. That it follows a pattern of being easy. Or even if not easy, being normal. Average. I never expected it to get more complicated than it was the day before. Never thought that after solving one problem, there would be another problem greater than the first one waiting to be solved. I hate this. This thing that life brings upon us. But the reason I hate it is that I always expect it to get easier.

However, I should always expect it to get harder. Who said things in life should be simple? Who said problems should not get compounded? In my profession, I constantly, on a daily basis, deal with other people's problems that get compounded. One comes in for the filling of a tooth and ends up needing a root canal and crown. Another comes in for a cleaning and finds out he will lose a tooth or need surgery. I mean, all of those people's lives are getting compounded on a daily basis, too. And I'm there for them to solve it. They can't solve it.

They come to me for help to solve the compounded problems.

But the problem with me is that I have to face my problems myself. I have to solve them myself. They are too great for others to handle. And I don't have the training to handle them, so I get overwhelmed. But the reason I get overwhelmed is not just that I don't have the means to solve them; I don't have the time or the patience to solve them. Or even to begin with, I feel that the problem should not exist. If I take upon myself a task, and it turns out to be complex, I feel that somebody is ganging up on me. Not realizing that it is in the nature of life to behave in the most complicated manner.

So, when I look back at my life now, it all seems very logical. It all falls into place. It is all right. There is no wrongdoing. There is no injustice. Life has been doing what it knows how to do best - behave in the most complicated manner. It all makes sense now. Why things happened when they did, how they did, what events they preceded, and what events followed. I always thought that something was wrong with life and that all of these things were happening the way they were happening. But hey, look at it here. Life has always been acting in its best form. It is doing its best to be as complicated as possible. Therefore, I do and should expect that any job that is undertaken is always going to meet hurdles and obstacles that make it more puzzling to solve. More difficult to sort and more painful to understand. It is all in the nature of life. If I try to make a trip reservation and they don't have the right time available or the right route, I should get happy and have praise for life because the game is being played right. Complications mean I am in flow with life, and I am winning the game of life. In the end, it will always be for the best.

So now we have put up our house for sale, and then a couple of weeks later, our neighbor puts up their house for sale at a cheaper price. And, of course, this makes matters harder for our house to get sold. And it even makes matters worse if we don't sell. Wow. What complexity has been created in this chess game? I knew it seemed too easy when I thought to myself that we would sell our house and move to a new house without hurdles. I should have expected the great moves life has up its sleeve. But I now know that these are not hurdles that life puts in my way. These are just the way things are. The way life itself has been trained to be. And it is acting in its best manner. Being a real challenge introducing as many complex issues in life as it can. What a game. Look at the challenges we face and overcome with our children. With their sickness. With their growth. With their scholastic progress. One complexity after another, and it works best when the complexities overlap to make a super giant compound thinking problem.

When the hurdles look their biggest and the complexities the most complex, that is when life has reached its ultimate efficiency. It is on its most routine road. Celebrate life as is.

CHAPTER 11
THE DRIVER WHO COULDN'T DRIVE
7/14/2001

I want to go places. I want to do things. I want to make things happen. I want to learn things. I want to achieve things. I want to gain things. I want to make a mark. I want to make people happy. I want to make me happy. I want to organize. I want to put things together. I want to satisfy my heart. I want to satisfy myself. I'm hungry for things to happen, but I don't make time or create opportunities for them to happen. I'm just wishing for things to happen. I'm just waiting to see things happen. I'm a driver with no steering wheel in my hand. I don't even have a gas pedal. The car just decides to go. And when it's going, I catch a ride, and I enjoy the ride, and when it stops, I stop with it. I have a steering wheel in my hand, but it does not steer to my command. I can't make it follow the road. I know the road, the direction to success and happiness, but I don't have the ability to steer towards it.

I push on the gas pedal, and the car takes off. But it doesn't go where I want it to go. It is so frustrating. I'm waiting for it to take me to my destination, and when I see I'm not getting close to my destination, I start to get mad. I make myself believe that I'm actually doing something and participating in the progress of my life, but all I'm doing is following the car that is on automatic pilot. It isn't on automatic pilot with a known program either; it is just going, and whoever gives it a push in the direction they want, it goes, and I go along with it. I don't steer, and I feel I can't steer, but I want to be the steerer because I feel I can steer in the right direction.

Why can't I just steer well? Where is my stamina, my go, my desire, my want, and my power? Why have I given up my right to steer? Why am I not taking us where I believe is the heaven waiting for us? Why can't I make a go of it? Why am I just sticking to the small things in life? I have so much to give, to explore, to invent and to produce. Why am I not taking charge of my life? I'm tired. I want happiness, so I have to make it work.

I've got to take control and act like the boss. I've got to take charge of my life. I've got to just do it to create something better. If it is to be, it is up to me.

Chapter 12
Is life supposed to have a meaning
12/27/2002

I have spent the last two years of my life trying to find out the meaning of life. To see what my purpose in life is. Why was I born, and what was I supposed to do? Am I here to serve somebody else? Am I supposed to do something to correct something in humanity or even in our own family? I am still as lost as I was two years ago. Mainly because I don't know if I can make any difference in people's lives. I wish I had the capability to steer people in the right direction, but my problem is that I don't know what the right direction is. Then I think to myself of what the prophets felt like. They were told they had a purpose in life. The message to them must have been very clear. They had to stir such uprisings. They had to influence people in such great ways. Where did they get their sure beliefs? How did they know what the right thing was to do? If they were mistaken with their beliefs, then a great disservice to humanity would have been committed. They must have been really sure of the message for them to have done something so big.

So here is where my confusion begins. If I have a purpose in life, the message to me is so unclear that I don't know what it is that I'm supposed to do. So, I am now beginning to think that I have no purpose in life. I am making too much out of nothing. I am here just because I am here and no more. I am here just like millions of other people to make something out of this life for myself. I am to enjoy this life because, in the end, nothing matters. When I'm gone, no one looks to see what I achieved in my life. I am too insignificant in the whole big picture to think I matter.

I must behave in a way that is insignificant to others. I am here just to make sense of my few rolls of the dice, just like a game of backgammon. When life ends, I will be nothing but a set of memories. If I dwell too much on figuring out what my purpose in life is, the memories that I may leave behind may not be as rosy as they would otherwise have been. It will be a picture with many flaws.

So, I came to the conclusion that my purpose in life is to live it as happily as I can and leave the best memories behind for my family and friends. I do not let anything of life bother me because life is too short, and who cares anyway?

CHAPTER 13
HAVE I BEEN HERE BEFORE
2/20/2003

The other night, I was over at the hospital visiting my brother, who had just had surgery on his leg. My cousin Mrs R was there too. My brother's wife, Leila, had just left a few minutes earlier, and my 10-year-old son and I were just waiting. I was waiting for it to become 9 o'clock so no more phone calls would come in while my brother was sleeping. All afternoon, people had been calling for their well wishes, not letting my brother get some much-needed rest.

Suddenly the phone rang, and for some reason, I thought it was Miss F (my other cousin). Yet it was actually Leila, who had just left, telling me to bring her phone down, and I thought it was Miss F, who, of course, refused since I didn't believe the phone belonged to her. At the end of the conversation, I still thought it was Miss F that I was talking to, and I told Mrs R to take Leila's phone down in case she was still in the parking lot. When they left, and now it was 8:55, I was staring at the phone, wishing it wouldn't ring since my brother had fallen asleep, and all of a sudden, it rang again. I picked it up hurriedly, almost before the first ring was halfway through ringing. This time, it was actually Miss F.

Why did I assume that it was Miss F when Leila had called earlier? Did I know from a previous experience in a different lifetime or a parallel life that Miss F was going to call that night? Hence, when the phone rang, I assumed it was Miss F even though there was no rhyme or reason as to why Miss F should be calling that time of the night. Have I been here before, or have I lived these experiences before?

Am I re-living life? How many times am I going to re-live this life, and is there something I am supposed to do that I am not doing and that is why I re-live it? Or is there some message I am supposed to get or deliver that I am missing each time that I re-live this life or experience? What is my role here, or do I even have a role? Do I know something that I need to share with someone or realize? Will I see something clearer if I pay more attention to my surroundings and the events around me? There is always something happening here. I should watch more closely. I should pay attention to life.

CHAPTER 14
THE LINE BETWEEN ECSTASY AND AGONY
3/7/2003

As the days travel by my eyes, I realize that this line between happiness and sorrow is getting thinner and thinner. The distance between these two moments in life is getting shorter, and jumping from one state of mind to the next becomes easier.

Does this make life better or less worthy? When I notice how easy it is to be happy one moment and totally satisfied with life, and then the next moment be engraved in the most debilitating pain in life and deep into sorrow, I lose all my respect for life. I know there were no guarantees in life, and there is no rule or logic to nature, but to see how content and happiness can be replaced by malice and fervor in the blink of an eye takes the preciousness of this world away. Is it that God gets bored sometimes and doesn't know what other good it can bring to stir up life that he all of a sudden decides to create a tragedy instead and watch the commotion that ensues, or is it just a random incident?

When I look closely, I see too much preciseness in this surgery to do the most damage for it to be considered incidental. When a surgeon takes the knife to the body, he plans first how he can make the best and deepest cut with the least strokes and the slightest tissue damage. He does not just jab at it. And this seems to be the preciseness that tragedies in our world hit. The operator looks to see where it is going to impact the most tak, es aims for it, and executes. Could it be just chance? No way I say, because I have seen too many innocent lives be interrupted to feel that there is any protection in place for the good people or to believe that only chance has taken its toll.

Or is it that the good people are the most conspicuous, and hence, life takes its hardest hits at them? Life does not see how much effort was put into developing this rose bush; it just takes its axe and cuts off the biggest and strongest branches down to the last knuckle. The tragic and sudden accidental loss of a dear friend, Dr P., has been a vivid example of the tyranny of life. How ruthless is the gardener? Who cannot see how many people get new life from the smell of the rose on this branch? How ruthless is it to take away the strongest branch and expect the rose bush to still perform its duty and give better flowers in the next season?

But if we knew there was a next season, and there was going to be a new bud on the stem, and there was going to be another flower as strong and beautiful as the original, maybe life's loss wouldn't be so painful. I am very sore from this loss, maybe as much as when I lost my mom. But if I knew that a new miracle was on its way, perhaps I could accept it easier.

CHAPTER 15
WHO ARE WE?
1/31/2004

I've always thought that mankind is the result of his experiences. But is it possible that I am wrong and that a person's experiences are the result of his thoughts, which then lead to who he /she is? Could it be that our thoughts guide the story of our life? Is it possible that what the mind imagines, the world creates?

So, let's see, professional soccer players have high self-esteem. They envision themselves scoring goals, making saves, playing in world competitions, and then it all happens right in front of our eyes.

Doctors envision healing their patients; they give them medicines and tell them they will get well. Those doctors who truly believe that their art heals people end up being good doctors and seeing good results. And those doctors who don't care about healing their patients and care about how much money they make end up with people who don't heal and get sicker and sicker, and so they end up making more money not because they wish bad for their patients, but because what they envision and imagine is something different than what the patient is there for.

Now, the monks envision tranquility and peace. They sit for hours meditating on peace, and then, of course, they experience it. Mountain climbers imagine reaching the top just because they want to, and then they do. And those who are not steadfast in their vision either don't reach the top or meet ill fate.

Are all the losers wavering in their visions, and that is why they lose? But then, if everybody envisioned winning, then we'd have to end up with a bunch of winners and no losers, but then how would that be possible? Could you have a soccer game in which both teams win because they were equal in what they saw in their future? Is that what a tie is, or could you actually have two winning teams at exactly the same time? Could Brazil and Germany both be World Cup champions in the same year when everyone over the world knows that only one of them took the Cup home? Or is it that somehow, over the course of the game, one team or its players start to see themselves beaten at the match, and so they lose?

So now, with the belief that what we think of and imagine creates our experience, I start to see a bright near future for myself and my family, one with great love, health, happiness, satisfaction, success, comfort, abundant wealth and love with my lovely immediate and extended family. I see every day as a bright day, one which is going to be full of goodness, and with the help, trust, and vision of God, what good I see comes to me.

CHAPTER 16
THE WINNING ATTITUDE OF A LOSER
2/25/2004

I can't help but start to think about the difference between a person who loses and knows he lost and feels he lost, a person who loses and knows he lost but doesn't feel he lost, and a person who loses but doesn't know he lost but feels like he lost, and finally, a person who loses but doesn't know he lost and doesn't feel that he lost. All of these are losers alike, but how the world around them shapes up is realistically going to be different.

Can one say which is better and which is worse? I think that the one who loses and feels he lost is the worst kind, and it really does not matter whether he knows he lost or not. The event of losing is a one-time event that, as soon as it happens, becomes a thing of the past and, therefore, obsolete. Losing is never in the future. And the people around us, even if they might remember that we, at some point in the past, lost, their judgment is valid only in the past tense. They cannot correctly judge our future, as we have many times seen sports forecasters' predictions be doomed.

It is up to us to present ourselves as losers or non-losers. It is how we *feel* that people will see. The experience in the past will have no chance to survive if we don't feel like a loser. Our attitude will radiate a message that will remind the people around us of the present moment to be experienced and not yet decided upon, and not what was in the past.

But also, this brings me to this thought that if we lose, and we don't know we lost, then automatically, we will not carry on a loser's mentality.

CHAPTER 17
OPTIMISTS THINK AND EXPECT THE BEST.
2/29/2004

I often think about what it means to be an optimist. Is it simply a train of thought, a mindset, or an action? Perhaps a set of actions leads to a positive result. Or does it even have to be a positive result? Is it simply enough to have the expectation of a positive result, regardless of the outcome, in order to be considered an optimist, or is it actually a prerequisite to have a positive outcome in order to be considered an optimist? The big question in my mind right now is whether the positive thinking in the optimist's train of thought actually leads to positive outcomes, and if one does not have this positive outlook, does it necessarily mean a positive outcome is unattainable?

I come about the scare tactics of many who say your experience follows your thought; therefore, if you think bad, then bad will happen, and if you think good, then good will happen. My personal experience says otherwise. If you think good and you expect good, two things happen. First, the fact that you expect the good puts you at a disadvantage because if the expectation does not meet reality, it propagates thoughts of failure. Second, expectation often exceeds actual reality, and the closer you get to your expectation, the further your expectation will travel, giving you the sense that you are never attaining a goal. Lastly, when you expect a Rose Garden and paint it the way you like or want it, when you get to the Rose Garden, if it is not painted the way you did in your mind, you feel you have not gotten to the Rose Garden, or that getting to the Rose Garden was not worth the work that it took because it is not what you expected.

If being in the Rose Garden does not furnish you with the good feeling you wanted to have when you got there, you actually might be in the Rose Garden, the best ever with the smelliest roses and most colorful that can be, but because it is not the one you imagined, you keep looking around, for your kind of rose garden. Then you are in a rose garden, and you are still working hard to get there, and you are saying, what the heck am I doing stuck over here in this mess, and you are trying to move on and struggling, yet this whole time you have been in the Rose Garden. Being present and paying attention to what is often clarifies the view, and we can see the Rose Garden we are in.

CHAPTER 18
IF I LOSE, I WIN
3/20/2004

Whenever I'm playing a soccer match or something else, I always worry about losing. This puts greater stress on me than necessary and makes me tired before I even start the competition. So now, all of a sudden, I think to myself, what if I create a scenario that even if I lose, I still win?

The original problem is that I always think there is one solution, one choice to win. And, of course, when that option is not achieved, I consider myself a loser and carry with it the stigma. But what if there is more than one option? What if I create a second option that even if I lose the game, there is something else I can have that I otherwise could not have had and create a winning proposition? In essence, losing now becomes a vehicle for winning the other good. A loss creates a path to have another want, and even though it is not the original want, the second want is so good that it can easily replace the original want.

It is not always easy to replace the original win with another win just as good, but I think a lot of times it can come pretty close. For example, when my son had a soccer game, I gave myself the option of going to Palm Springs if he lost since there wouldn't be a next game, so now he either wins, which is great, or he loses, which means we then go to Palm Springs and have a blast of a time and give him a good time and we still win.

It is up to us to always create a win for ourselves despite the chance of loss in something else.

CHAPTER 19
WHEN THE END IS NOT IN SIGHT
6/27/2004

Many times, we start down a path with a road map and an end in sight. We make a plan and start a journey and make plans and follow directions, and we can see what the end is going to be like and what it is going to bring us. And after a certain amount of work and time spent and days passing by, we get to what we had imagined to be.

But there are times that no matter how much planning we can do and how perfect we choose a path, the end does not appear clear, and we don't know where we are going to end up and what it is going to be. We try to choose the best path and work the hardest to make the best, but the end looks questionable, and we feel that we are losing the game and the battle, and we feel we are not getting anywhere. We don't know what the end is going to look like, and often, we see a surprise outcome that we could not have ever guessed or imagined, sometimes good and sometimes bad.

What has to be, though, is that you have to trust in the future and in the good of life, that in the end, he who has been righteous and kept a vision of the goal he had in mind without wavering from his own positive and beneficial will, somehow fulfills his purpose in life and reaches where he wants to be and where he is meant to be to bring his best life forward. The timing may be a little different from what was in mind, but we must trust that it will happen.

Sit tight and do your work, and then all of a sudden, you will see you are sitting on a high spot on top of the world, and you will laugh at the journey you had to take to get where you are. The ups and downs of the journey don't matter because there are always obstacles that catapult one to the next step closer to the desired goal.

CHAPTER 20
DOES HEAVEN HAVE TO WAIT?
11/14/2004

Recently, this question came to my mind when asking one of my friends: "If you were told that you could go to heaven with full benefits the way you always imagined heaven would be, would you be willing to leave everything behind and go right now." Or would you even have to leave everything behind and go on in order to feel that you are in heaven? Would you be willing to exchange yours NOW for a direct pass to the heaven you have imagined?

I started to think. Heaven is a pretty big offer. That is cool. That is the ultimate destination anyone would want. That is what everyone always works towards, and that would be pretty cool if it was offered to me right now. But then the questions started to pour in. Is this going to heaven a permanent thing, or does it have a time limit? If it has a time limit, what happens afterward? Do I start from the beginning, or do I start from where I left off? What benefits will I be able to carry over from heaven into the next phase?

Then, I also started to think about the things you would leave behind when you were going to heaven. What will happen to them, their family, and their friends, and what feelings will they go through? Does it matter what they go through since you are going to heaven anyway? I mean, let's really think what the cost of victory is, victory being winning a soccer game or going to heaven. If the game is won at all costs, then it really does not matter what happens to everybody else; what matters is with whom and when and for how long the trophy will end up.

But what if it matters what happens to the others (spectators, coaches, clients, team managers, friends, family) because these are the same people that you will have to carry future games with, and they are going to be instrumental in your experiences the next time you are not in heaven, or even when they arrive in your heaven.

After I had explored all these options about going to heaven and picking heaven over the NOW, I thought to myself: if I have heaven right now, if this is heaven, if I have created heaven for myself, and if my experiences represent the experiences I would be subject to in heaven, then would there even be a need for going to heaven. In other words, can there be heaven on earth? Can I create my own heaven right here, right now? What needs to be present for me to feel that heaven is here right now?

And then the real question comes: Do I really have heaven at my disposal right now? Look around and open your eyes. Do I really see heaven around me? And if not, is heaven really around me, and it's just that I am not seeing and recognizing it? And if heaven is not really around me, with what there is around me, can I create heaven around me? Can I imagine this heaven in my head and then experience it, and then create it so it exists for me? Am I the creator of my heaven, or is there a test I have to pass to feel and experience heaven? Can I and should I accept what is my best heaven yet, love it, live it the way it is as best as I can, and cherish the moments as if it is the best heaven has to offer?

CHAPTER 21
THE NEW SOUL
12/12/2004

A few weeks ago, my brother-in-law brought a new puppy to our house, which he had found in the street. It was very weird. Almost immediately, the puppy felt connected to us, and we felt connected to the puppy. He looked at us with eyes that seemed to be talking. He couldn't talk, but words seemed to be pouring out of his light brown eyes. I don't know exactly what he was trying to tell us, but there was one thing for sure: he had a way of communicating with me like no other dog had before. I have been getting a lot of messages from across the border of life, and I'm not sure what it all means and what I am to make of it all, but somehow, the decision-making that seemed to be very hard is becoming easier. Somehow, things seem to want to make their purpose clear.

So I've thought to myself, what if this all means there is a communication from the afterworld? Should I take this as a sign that things are on their way to finally get better? Do the "God Winks" that I see mean anything? Am I supposed to do anything?

For now, I just look around and see that this dog has the intelligence of a grown-up dog, is being kind to our family, and is bringing a lot of joy to our house. My son seems to be very keen about keeping the dog. Interestingly, even the name that has come to me for this dog raises thoughts. I named him "Funny" because that is what his eyes tell me to call him. And whenever I call him, I feel happiness when I call out Funny. He listens to me and obeys well when commanded to. Almost as if he is some soul that needs to be near us for a time to watch us and finish some unfinished business. Or maybe he is just spending some open unused time wisely till the right time comes for the right move.

He sure can't talk now and can't give away any secrets of life. I won't have the answers now and may never have the answers, but maybe someday I'll look back, and things will make sense, and the pieces of the puzzle will fall into place. Not everything has a meaning or a purpose, but it may be that in the totality, there is wisdom in what we've taken in. Maybe it is just the love that we needed to have around us and was missing for a while. Maybe it was the ability to just be more playful and not take life so seriously. We just need to become part of the game of life and flow with it.

CHAPTER 22
THE IMPOSSIBLE
3/22/2005

As I'm contemplating my trip to Lake Tahoe for a ski trip with my kids tomorrow, I can't help but think about what are the possibilities for something that is impossible to happen. If it's impossible, it only means that it hasn't happened before, right? Or does it also mean that it cannot happen in the future, or does it merely mean that there is a chance of it happening? It hasn't happened before, and it is waiting for a good time to happen, and if you dream it, it will happen.

Who is prone to meet impossible events or have impossible achievements overcome by their efforts. It is the end of March, and spring started three days ago. We are going on vacation, and there is a big winter storm in California, where normally warm weather arrives early. What were the chances of something like this to happen to a normal person? So if this person is a person who attracts all these impossibilities, isn't it then possible that by virtue of definition, this person will also be a person who will discover some impossible means or way of doing something and will achieve something that was thought to be impossible?

So, as I'm sitting on the couch and contemplating on my "misfortune" of having to travel in a snowstorm when I expected to have warm sunny skies and spring skiing conditions in Tahoe, I start to think whether I should stress out over the facts of what kind of trouble I will go through to get to my destination, or I just have to lean back and know that this world is full of surprises and impossibilities and each impossibility paves the way to conquer an obstacle and reach higher levels of pleasure and enjoyment. To know the end result is what will give the message of how a person should feel when presented with a challenge.

The end result is what will build one's stamina and zeal to succeed.

It is a few days later now, and we ended up going on that trip despite the severe winter storm that was hitting northern California during Spring. It seemed impossible for us to get through the shutdown Freeway because of a major accident, but suddenly the impossible became possible when I told the person who was turning all the cars around back to Reno, where my destination was. Fortunately, my exit was just before where the traffic pileup was on the mountain road. We made it through a winter storm and a traffic blockade, got to our hotel, and had the most beautiful and amazingly wonderful time. The end result made all the worry and fears worthless and disappear. Strength replaced weakness, but I am the one who had to take a chance and follow through with my plan and dream. Glad I did.

CHAPTER 23
ARE THE CHILDREN A PREVIEW OF OUR FUTURE LIFE
5/9/2009

Sometimes, I come to think of it: Am I making my children's lives up by my actions, or are my children's lives a preview of what the oneness and higher being have designed for me and is giving me a glimpse of it? I look at my two children, and I see two worlds. Different ones. One is always high on winning and getting what he wants and making his wishes come true, and the other one really works hard. The harder that child works, the less she is rewarded, and she is always put to the maximum test with the obstacles that are put in the way.

Then I think of my own life. It can be so easy, and yet it is so hard. It seems that I am living the life of my children simultaneously in one body. Is this a message for me that is trying to tell me, "Hey, look at what works and what needs to be done," and give me a hint of what I should and should not stress out for? Is it showing me a path to choose for my own life? Or is it trying to help me come up with answers for them and help them win their lives?

If I change something in my life, will that child that is the projection of that part of my life change? Will his or her experiences also take a different course?

If something in my life is an obstacle and a bother, if I work to overcome it and win my way with it, will I all of a sudden see that the child who is a reflection of that side of me sees and experiences success and prosperity? Are my children a mirror of my life? Am I seeing in the mirror what I am, what my troubles are, and what my strengths are? Hence, I must use this information to better myself and recreate the life that my children are experiencing. In other words, is it a circle of actions and reactions?

I am not sure if the sufferings and disappointments that my children experience are a result of my actions and personal life experiences. Could it somehow be that if I fix something in my life, my children will automatically see and experience an improvement in their lives? Could it possibly be a two-way street? That is to say, when I fix some hangup that they have in their life, all of a sudden, I will experience the doors of success and opportunity open in that department of my life, too. Could it be true that in helping my children overcome their fears, I am directly influencing my own life and making myself live a better life? A race car, no matter how good an engine, will drive as well as the tires can perform and as good as the driver is, so if we fix the tires, will the car stand a better chance of navigating the course of life successfully?

Sometimes, no matter how good the tires are, you need an engine overhaul, and if you do that, you will suddenly see the capability of the high-grade tires to perform. Indeed, it is a two-way street.

CHAPTER 24
THE SECRET OF THREE 1'S OR 111
10/15/2005

A while back, about a year ago, a thought came to my mind, a message, kind of a deal, that when I came across three 1's, something big was going to happen, and in my mind, something big either meant going to heaven or seeing heaven here on earth and that by virtue of winning a lottery, because in my life the only thing that was missing was financial wealth that I had not achieved. The dealer inferred to me that when I see 111 in repetition in my days, it means I am getting closer and closer to the day of winning.

So it all started as a fun thing, and I started to notice the three 1s. They appeared on my odometer, on car license plates stopped in front of me, on my clock, on ticket stubs, and so on.

Then we went to Hawaii, and I shared half of the story about 1s with my two children, who are in their teens now, but I didn't tell them what it was supposed to signify. Then we started to see it on food bills, on room numbers, etc. The funniest thing was that one night after we had gone through a sequence of room changes that were not good in a hotel that we were staying at in Hawaii, we were in front of a jewelry store, and we got into a conversation about the Presidential Suite at the hotel which had a sign on the wall where we were standing. The next day, as we were getting out of our room to go on a tour, the concierge called us and said they had mistakenly moved us to our current room and they needed it back. And because of their mistake, they were going to move us to a better room. In the afternoon, when I went with the kids to get our key, we were told that our room was #1114, the presidential suite. What a coincidence, three 1's. Of course, the room was a dream place overlooking the ocean, with a balcony, huge Jacuzzi, dining area, and stereo system. The stay was heavenly.

We came back from our trip and got ready for my son's Bar Mitzvah. Saturday, October 1, was his Torah reading. When the Rabbi announced the page number in the living Torah for the Torah portion, I was awe-stricken. Page 1101. So now I was sure I was winning the lottery. Then, I realized that I was also in heaven. Nine years after a series of unfortunate events, I am sitting in the Sephardic Temple, watching my son being a Bar Mitzvah carrying the Torah and reading from the Torah with my daughter sitting next to me after I had beaten cancer against all odds.

Yes, at that moment, I was in heaven, and the 111 was a sign that I was on the right track with God watching over me and carrying me through the steps of my life. I was being in the right place, at the right time, doing the right thing. The 0 in there was the miracle zero, that which, even with nothingness, makes all the difference.

CHAPTER 25
WHAT'S IN A FACE
9/6/2007

Has it ever been that you look at somebody and just because of the way they look or how they appear or present themselves, you make a judgment about them and then mistreat them or slack off in giving them the service they really deserve only because they are not as beautiful as the other customers or people you deal with? Well, today, I came across a situation that made me think about who I am and who I can be.

I was providing services to this old lady. She doesn't look attractive, nor does she dress well. The way she actually presents herself every time she comes to me makes me think twice about why I am in the profession I am. But today, while I was working on her, all of a sudden, I had a passing thought. What if the almighty has placed the most important soul into my hands, whether in this lifetime or from a previous one, into this body that's in front of me right now just to test my integrity? To see how righteous I am in treating others and how high on the ladder of divinity I have climbed or can climb.

I took a second look at this woman and noticed how much sympathy I would have offered her if she were a close soul to me. I somewhat felt shameful, and in an instant, I realized how ruthlessly I must have been acting toward this person who may be present in this world as somebody not so attractive. I realized how poor my judgment could have been to just think of this person based on what she looked like. Can you imagine how our world would change if when we look at a face, and we decide we don't like it, or even we hate it, we would actually be able to unravel the façade and see the soul that was residing in that body and see that it is the soul of a beloved perhaps? It's a bit magically supernatural, but it's possible.

So I say, next time you try to make a decision as to how to treat someone else because of their looks, color, what they are wearing, or how they speak, be cognizant of the fact that what you see is not what is there, it might actually be a part of your own soul that you are treating and decide to do the right thing and treat it as if that person is housing your most precious and admired soul.

CHAPTER 26
EXPECTATIONS
1/28/2006

Recently I took a trip abroad. Full of expectations to do certain things, go certain places, and achieve certain things. I had it all pictured in my mind. I knew what I wanted and what I should have. After all, isn't that what it is supposed to be? What you picture is what will be, and what you get?

Then, during the trip, from day to day, I was the victim of unmet expectations. There was a certain part of the town that I used to remember was a happening place, and then when we went there, it turned into a deserted place. No one was there. Where shops, music, and galleries used to be the rule of the day now stood empty walkways. The next day, I expected to have a ceremony in a very spiritual setting; I had hyped up myself to meditate and connect with the source, but instead, what was set up was a very beautiful ceremony in a very beautiful tent, which did not allow you to devour the surrounding atmosphere. I kept on having expectations about things, and every time it didn't happen, I found a reason to feel unsatisfied, down, or complaining, making me unable to enjoy even what was there.

Then I stopped having expectations, and wow, all of a sudden, things were so much prettier. As I came to each new place, I started to see something beyond my dreams. It was like reading a new book or watching a movie for the first time. I learned my lesson, and that was to have no expectations. Wants and desires, maybe. But no expectations. If you expect, you can set yourself up for failure, anger, dissatisfaction, and frustration. If you desire, you always leave room for improvement, get fulfilled without the chance of failure, and give yourself a chance to enjoy what there is and where you are because no matter where you are, it is much better than where somebody else is or something else that could have been. Expectation only puts you at a disadvantage point.

It does seem very hard not to have expectations because, after all, we have become used to depending on certain things in life. We expect our cars and computers to work when we want to switch them on, our kids to perform the way we want, and our spouses and relatives to do things that make us happy. We expect life, our earth, and the sunrise all to be there the next day. Nature has taught us to have expectations. But if we can accept that nothing, even the sun, can not be expected to be there the next day, then nothing is going to matter because there will be nothingness, and then we realize that having expectations is unreasonable.

Having wants is good, but don't let that desire turn into a carving in the rocks of expectation.

CHAPTER 27
CHANGE
3/2007/2006

Once Upon a time, I was proud to be a stable person. I used to take pride in being able to maintain things the way they were. Prevent change. Keep steady. Stay with the old, the routine, the norm, the usual. I stayed in the same school for 12 years, went to a stinky college in a city that I didn't like for four years, and didn't think about transferring to a better college (actually not; I did try to transfer to Yale now that I remember), stayed in the same apartment with my mom for eight years, bought a house and stayed 13 years, rented a home and stayed four years, became a dentist and got into two offices and stayed with the same set up for 19 years, kept the same employees, etc...... I was either afraid to change and create change or even took pride in keeping the status quo, being proud to maintain it. Now, however, I am coming to the conclusion that what I thought of as a positive asset was probably the most destructive force in my life.

I now believe that the more change one might have in their early childhood, given that it is not because of bad events, and the more used they get to adapting to the new and giving up the old for experiencing and experimenting with something new, the better fit for life one will be. That is the essence of success: to be able to see your surroundings change and change with it rapidly, to take advantage of the opportunities that come along even though they appear as creating discomfort, take them on with an open heart, accept the challenge, and create change and go with the flow of the river, and during the journey, find a good bank to shore up your boat along the river and build up a new camp.

I also see that as one gets older, it gets harder to view change as positive and accept or create change. It probably is a good teaching to get someone used to change and its effects and stimulate one's ability to cope with change in their younger years as much as possible so the fear of change does not block the path to the future.

I have come to realize that even the biggest institutions change: the Presidency, the banks, and the supermarket chains, and they all land in a better spot when they change. Even though the change involves reorganization and cost, they plan and then implement.

This ideology has even inhibited me in my work, where I am sometimes hesitant to create change in people's smiles. I look for excuses to dissuade them from doing it and push them into keeping the status quo, whereas they may actually be wanting to get something different, and I can help them get there. I need to learn that change does not mean ruining the past or the present; it only means that you want the future to be different, maybe more in tune with the path of life, as a change in that path is inevitable.

CHAPTER 28
LUCK
1/11/2007

Ever wondered what luck is? Or rather, good luck. Because there is bad luck, too.

What is good luck?

It is coming across a good result despite having made bad decisions and initial signs that things are not going right. But when we made the decisions, did we know they were bad, or were we sure they were good? If we were sure it was a good decision, then between then and now, something strange must have happened to make us feel that it was the wrong decision. Things such as bad outlooks. Something that would make us scared, something that would make us have shattered beliefs. And so we start to expect something scary, and then all of a sudden things turn out right, and voila, you end up in the right spot, then you say to yourself that wow, despite that wrong decision that I made, things turned out right. Or do you say, boy, I always knew I would make the right decisions?

But what if you were not sure of the decision you were making and you just decided to do something not knowing what the outcome might be and what might come up, and then soon after, you would say," Oh shit, I was wrong," and then some time passes, and then one day you wake up, and you see all is well, and everything is perfect despite the wrong decision you made. That is what good luck is, because you had no basis on what you made your decision, and initially, you were proved wrong, and then, with a turn of events, you were declared the winner. That had nothing to do with your effort, knowledge, or ability; it was just the way the world turned. Sometimes it turns in the right direction, and sometimes not.

Which one results in greater happiness? The right decision turned out right, as you expected, or apparently, the wrong decision turned out right as you would not have expected. Is it the expectation that leads to happiness or the surprise? Then, on top of all this, if you look at the statistical chances and probabilities that several wrong decisions would turn out right, how do you react? Do you start to trust yourself more, or do you start to trust the universe more? It surely increases your confidence. So good luck can bring a better connection between you and the universe, and vice versa. Can a better connection with the universe bring good luck, or is there any relation between the two?

Maybe it requires a bit of attention to see which is the case and then follow the lead.

CHAPTER 29
WHY CHOOSE TO LIVE
2/10/2007

Have you ever asked yourself:" When I die, will I have access to God and the heavens?" of course, granted that one has lived with integrity and love for self and others and ethics and lack of wrongdoing and with the love of God and for all its children.

Then why do we sometimes choose to forgo the calling of God and fight our removal from this earthly world and decide to stay on, knowing that the continued life here will perhaps bring more misery to our personal lives? We will face harsh obstacles, we will lose our valor, taste many defeats, and maybe become removed from our destiny and purpose, and be subject to further humiliation by life.

Is it our commitment to others, our children, spouses, parents, or siblings, that takes precedence over our flight to the path of freedom, or is it that we have a bigger calling? One that propels us to live longer to fulfill and accomplish certain tasks or promote certain events. Often, it seems to me that it is a result of a commitment or the perception of having a commitment to another, and this is more evident in individuals who, throughout their lives, have shown greater commitment to others and those who have given their lives for the benefit of a few. You see how the world's greatest philanthropists live the longest lives, for example, Mother Teresa, but at the same time, we see that great women like Princess Diana leave prematurely. Is this premature departure a result of great personal pain that one is suffering in their current life and hence decides to leave despite their will to promote an idea in the world, or is it that they have a bigger calling, and they need to leave and come back in reincarnation as a figure that can do more good than in their present body. When one tries to achieve a task and, because of his/her position in life, is unable to, the time comes when it becomes highly desirable to leave and return in a form that one can achieve the primary goal in a better manner. Or maybe it is only to relinquish their position in life to another who may be able to do what they want to be done. Then, allow their soul to travel to the free world and taste the sweetness of the company of his/her God and the peacefulness and serenity of the heavens.

It is not our position to question this departure, whether it was for the sole selfish purpose of freeing oneself from the commitments of this earthly life, for allowing room for another to blossom, or for returning as a more influential character. When one sees that he/she has achieved what needs to be done and has cared for and taken care of those who depend on one's being, then and only then can the departure be considered a blessed one, and it should be welcomed and not grieved.

The sense of loss does bring sadness with it, but the greater sense of one's ability to manifest his/her greater goal and want must be considered and respected and welcomed with the greatest acceptance because it is only then that the departed soul can rest freely and proclaim its journey into life a victory.

CHAPTER 30
A GLIMMER OF HOPE
2/16/2007

I had been going through one of the most depressing times of my life. Not because I lost someone or have had a disease, but because I felt I no longer had a place in this world. I was lost and had been so humiliated that I didn't care anymore. I kept going through the days, a minute at a time, hoping that the strength of my internal powers would enable me to overcome this tragedy and convince me that there was usefulness to me.

Days went by, and no such thing happened. Later in the week, it was Friday afternoon, and my receptionist came and told me that this lady called from New York and said that she was a friend of my mom, and her name was Butterfly, and that she loved me a lot.

At first, I was bewildered. Who is Butterfly in New York? Why just call me and say what she said? What have I done? Or not done. What had happened? Was something coming up? Should I be ready for something? It was even more interesting because all of a sudden, I remembered the word butterfly from when I was going to my therapist, how in one of the sessions, the butterflies came up in my visions, and then when I went to this lecture at a hotel to hear Deepak Chopra, he was signing and selling his book named "The secret of life" and it had a picture of a butterfly on the cover. When I asked him if that was just by chance or if it actually had a meaning, he responded that the cover was going to be something else, and then some event made him change it to the butterfly.

So, all of a sudden, out of all my disappointments, just because of this phone call, I was motivated.

Later, I guessed the identity of this person when I translated her name to Farsi, Parvaneh, and it then became even more unusual why this person had called me with that message. She was a very Godly person, intellectual and spiritual, whom my mother admired and trusted a lot. Was this a message from the heavens? I don't know, but I do know that somebody in this world cares about me. Somebody whom I have never benefited, done anything for, said a kind word to or helped. This somebody was my glimmer of hope.

CHAPTER 31
THE OLD MAN WHO CAME TO DINNER
2/17/2007

Years ago, I remember that my Mom used to invite this old man who used to live in the condominium next to ours in the building. He was very frail and old. Could hardly see or walk but was a very eloquent speaker. She would invite him on Shabbat dinners and on Passover when only my brother and sister were there. I would wonder to myself why my mom was inviting this old man to our house. I know he is a very nice and likable man, but this is a close family get-together. Nonetheless, my mother would invite him every so often, and I could never understand why.

Then, a few weeks ago, on one of the nights when we were having a Shabbat dinner at my house, my mother had passed on about ten years. The doorbell rang, and as I opened the door, I saw my in-law's grandfather, a very old and frail man, working his way slowly from the car to our doorstep. He would come every so often to our house when we had gatherings for Shabbat. As he was walking, out of my cold-heartedness, I thought to myself, what motivation did this old man have to go through all this trouble to come here? And out of my selfishness, I asked myself what was in it for me.

It didn't take more than 2 seconds for this noble thought to come to my mind, though. What if my mother's soul has a chance to live through this old person, and that is a way for her to find her way to my house on Shabbats now that I miss her presence so much? What if the reason my mother was inviting that first old man to our house was that, somehow, she could connect with her parents, who had been long gone?

Then I asked myself if this could even remotely have a chance to be true; this old man could be carrying part of my mother's or father's soul, and through him, I may be able to feel them. I suddenly felt a great deal of passion. I could see the love in his eyes. I could see their eagerness to come and visit us for Shabbat in his eyes. Tears started to roll down the corner of my eyes, and when this old man arrived at my doorstep, I gave him the biggest hug. I felt so good. And I could tell he felt the warmth of my hug.

Now, it didn't even matter anymore whether he had part of my mom's soul in him or not. I loved having him.

CHAPTER 32
AN INTERVIEW
3/11/2007

Interviewer: So tell me, what do you think of the years you lived in Beverly Hills?

K: We moved there and rented a house. This house wasn't exactly what I hoped to live in after I had remodeled my house in Brentwood's best location, but it seemed like a good move. It was so old and run down. I was happy that my children were going to go to the Beverly Hills school system. The streets looked nice and clean. The sun was brighter, and it was nice to walk around the streets and not have to deal with the cold ocean breeze that was always present in Brentwood, where our previous home was.

I: How do you compare this with the times you went out for a walk at your old house?

K: My children were younger back then, so everything was different. We would often go for a walk, especially on Sunday nights. We'd go to a restaurant down the street and walk back, or sometimes we would drive. Ever since we moved out here, we haven't done that. Everybody is out doing their own thing. Even though we are very close to places, we never walk to a restaurant. The home seems nice and big, so we are a lot more comfortable eating in the house. Also here we have a lot more friends. So we end up eating with them or at their house a lot. Or my kids go to their houses, so I just end up doing my own cooking.

I: How are your mood and attitude these days after living four years in Beverly Hills?

K: Well, this little city is very beautiful, and the streets are all nice. But what it boils down to is that I look around me, and everybody has at least doubled their equity during these years, just because they had a house, and because I didn't buy a house, my equity didn't rise at all, and aside from that, my return on my money was very low. That hurts. Every morning, I get up and look at the world as a new, bright place. I do my things, take the kids to school and go to work, put a hard day in, and run run run all the time, chasing time the whole time, losing track of my sanity and self. And then, at the end, I raise up my head and look, and I see that I've landed 10 yards back. Even when I make investments, hoping to gain something, I look, and I see pretty much all of my choices have taken a nosedive, even in a good market. I am starting to think: "Dear God, is there any kindness you can bestow upon me."

I look up to God and pray and give my thanks and gratitude, and I hope that there is a little bit more of goodness that can come my way. Yes, I do count my blessings, my home, good bed, good children, and good life, and I give many thanks for all that God has brought my way. But what I ask is that it is possible that once in a while, God will throw in a little bonus for me. I mean every hard-working employee deserves a little bonus. I guess that is what I am looking forward to.

I: So if I would tell you that you are not going to get any bonuses while you are looking to get it, and the bonus will come when it decides and wants to come, what do you feel?

K: I will keep on going around doing my thing. When the bonus shows up in my life, I will take it in with open arms. I guess it is stupid to ruin my day now, trying to wait for the bonus. I mean, look how beautiful it is outside. This time is going to go by and not come back. If I spend it waiting for the bonus, time is gone. I will say hello to life and live it well, expecting nothing but desire something fuller and better. In time, good things will come my way. I know it. So, I am not going to ruin my day now, questioning why and thinking how else it could have been. I will accept what is. What is is still very good compared to what is elsewhere. I accept my blessings.

I will always say that I am happy, and I hope that when I look back some years from now, I remember those as good old times and be satisfied that I got the most out of it when I could.

CHAPTER 33
WHY I DON'T HAVE PLANS
5/21/2007

Recently, I have been thinking to myself as to why things don't work out for me. Why does it seem I am not ready for events and world and life? I always used to pre-plan everything. I was ready for events. I had a plan for everything, whether it was vacation, my children's school, things to do, or purchases. For everything, I had a plan. Additionally, it seemed that I had the blueprint for every plan in my head so that when the time for decision-making arrived, it was easy and quick. I was ready for things. But recently, it seems that I am not prepared for things; I am often caught off guard. I am not ready for things when they happen. Events come and go without me being ready for them, and I often miss things that I should have done at certain times in order for certain things to work for me in the future. It seems I am not prepared anymore. I don't have the solutions to problems ready in my head. All new events look foreign to me, as if it is the first time I have come across this situation, and it takes me a long time to digest and analyze events and come up with an appropriate decision, and then often, the decision is not even the right one. Or at least it is not the decision with the most advantages and least disadvantages.

So today, I started to think about how my mind has taken this turn in life. Why am I not prepared? Why is my intuition not working anymore? Why am I not able to make fast, quick decisions?

Suddenly, this thought came to my mind. When I was created, and my destiny was preprogrammed and designed, I was not supposed to be here at this point in my life. I was not supposed to have survived this long. My designed mind was never programmed to have a calendar of events for the years 1996 (when I got cancer) and later.

It seems that I was not supposed to have survived the awful cancer, and somehow, when through some miracle, my life was saved, everything went awry because none of these dates existed in the calendar anymore, and no preprogramming was made. Simply put, I was not supposed to be here at this point in time, so my destiny files had no predetermined files encoded in them. So now, when I come to choice points, I have nothing to go by. I have to start fresh to think, judge, and decide, and my memory has no database in it to depend on for making good, solid, and correct decisions.

So now that I know all of this, I feel more comfortable with myself. It is not that I have to feel bad when it takes time to decide and I am not ready for events and I get totally flabbergasted by events; it is just the way life is and was supposed to be; it is just that I don't belong here and I am here just by virtue of luck or necessity as an added bonus for being a survivor, and all I need to do is do my best and deal with things one thing at a time. I should make new plans and make a new track for guiding myself to new successes in my new days of life that are coming as a bonus.

I should feel powerful because now since there is no written destiny, I can create new experiences and destinies with my thoughts and my visions.

CHAPTER 34
THE UPS AND DOWNS OF THE MONTH OF JUNE
6/12/2007

When June begins, I enter into an emotional roller coaster. I don't know what to be. Happy, angry, sad, frustrated, determined, thankful, gracious, resentful, faithful, oblivious, trusting. All these thoughts and emotions are valid and applicable to this month.

I started to believe that it was a good month because I married my love on June 11 and bought my first house on June 13 of the following year, but then 13 years later, in June, I sold that house and entered the stage of my life where I suffered the biggest financial loss of my life when prices of the houses doubled, and I had no house.

In June, my son was born, the pride of my life and a great surprise and blessing from God; in the month of cancer, I also had surgery to remove a cancer from my body, a cancer that was on track to kill me in June. So, I was very joyous to find out that the cancer had not spread to any other part of my body, and I had a blast at my niece's Wedding on June 21, but then the next day, I found out that I had to have chemotherapy, the kind of chemotherapy that turned out to blow the life out of me. So, by the end of June, I started preparations for chemotherapy, something that probably saved my life but took precious time of life away when my mother passed away just as June ended in the following year. So now, when the Hebrew calendar moves around every year, the anniversary of my mother's passing almost always falls on some significant day in June, sometimes it is Father's Day, sometimes my son's birthday, sometimes my wedding anniversary, sometimes graduation days, and sometimes just a day in June.

At times, I wished I could erase the memory of the month of June from my mind, but then with it would go all the good memories of the month of June. Is it worth the trade-off, the sacrifice, the wait to see what's next?

I wonder to myself how I can overcome these ups and downs, how I can function like a normal person and make the best, at least for my kids, so they remember the month of June as a good month. I sure hope that something really good and really big happens in June so that we can remember it as that and celebrate each June day as it is now and not for what it was in the past.

CHAPTER 35
THE GIVING HAND
7/5/2007

I was going to be going to Cancun, the land of beauty and beaches, for a summer vacation. It was going to be beautiful, I thought to myself. I am going to have a great time. It is going to be a great program at Club Med, and we will have dancing and fun. But then, as usual, I started to think of the poor gardeners who have to work in the heat of the summer to keep the plants and the flowers healthy and beautiful. I thought of the hurricane that had destroyed the land, caused so much headache and damage, and ruined the hard work of so many workers. I started to feel sorry for all those workers who had to do the thankless hard work of maintaining the place. Nobody ever recognizes these people, I thought to myself, but that club would not be as beautiful as it should be if it weren't for these people.

So I went to the bank, changed $200 into $10 bills, and told myself that as I was walking through the beautiful grounds on my vacation, I would just start to give these bills away to the hard workers in the heat of the day. When we got there the next morning, I woke up early, as usual, and went out for a stroll by myself. I stuffed a couple of the bills into my bathing suit pocket just in case I ran into anybody to whom I thought I should give the money, hoping that they would feel thanked for the job they did. I came across a couple of workers who were digging up weeds under the hot morning sun. I almost reached into my pocket, but I shied away. It was almost as if I didn't have the courage to do what I planned to do. I walked by them and went about my activities, paying little attention to what had gone through my mind.

The next day, again, I tried, and it was as if I was looking for excuses not to do what I had dreamt about doing. In all honesty, what I wanted to do was a good thing, but I don't know why I was hesitant, and I would again and again shy away from doing it. The next day, I passed by one and then another gardener, each time trying to make a decision about why I should and why I shouldn't give the money to this person or the other. Finally, I came to my senses. I said to myself I have this money in my pocket, and I am not going home with it, so I might as well start to give it away. So, I reached into my pocket and took one of the $10 bills out, said hello to this old man who was attending the flowers, thanked him for keeping the flowers beautiful, and handed him the money. Granted, it wasn't a whole lot of money, but the smile on the wrinkled face of that man who expected nothing that day but the impact of the scorching sun on his back was unforgettable. Somehow, all of a sudden, it became easier to give. I came across another guy and did the same, this time with more pleasure than fear. Maybe fear of hurting their pride in what they were doing.

The next day, I was out to give out more bills. I had started to become choosy about who to give the money to. I ruled out one lad because it seemed to me that he was talking to his friend more than paying attention to the weeds and passed by another, thinking that he didn't need the money because his clothes looked too new and clean compared to the others.

Later that evening, the same happened; this younger lad was watering the trees, kind of in a shady area, and again, I was going to walk away from him, using as an excuse the fact that it wasn't too hot and the guy didn't seem to be sweating enough to deserve the money.

Then I thought to myself, who am I to make a judgment as to who deserves and who does not? How can I give this responsibility to myself to make one person happy and not the other one? Who am I to decide who benefits? I realized what I was doing was completely wrong, becoming the decision-maker of who to give to and for what reasons. I was out there just to give. So, I just walked out there to the young lad in the shade and started to talk in my broken Spanish language, inquiring about the trees that he was watering. Most of them had been uprooted during the hurricane, he explained, so now they are replanting them. I gradually reached for one of the bills and handed it to him, thanking him for doing such a beautiful job in making the beauty come back to the village. Again, I saw the same smiling face, being happy that someone had recognized what he was doing instead of just walking by. From that point on, it was easy.

By the end of the next day, I had handed out all the bills. It felt good. It felt good knowing that no one expected them yet; maybe it made a few people think, thank you. I could only hope that those bills that I handed out would give the recipients at least a few minutes of joy because what I had received in return was far more valuable than the satisfaction that comes with expressing gratitude and giving.

CHAPTER 36
HOW MY LIFE DOES NOT CEASE TO AMAZE ME
7/24/2007

It has been a while since unusual events took place in my life. Events that were totally unexpected and uncalled for. Real shockers. Mom's accident, my tumor, Mom's sudden death. Father-in-law's 1st cancer and then fast death from 2nd cancer, all in a matter of 3 years. I thought my shockers were over. But I see that events are happening daily that shock me. Maybe not of the same magnitude, but the shock effect is still there.

For example, how all stocks go up, and all of a sudden, the stock that I had takes a nose dive. How as soon as I sell my house, the prices of houses go up, and then, to top it off, where I want to buy a house, the prices jump 200%, and elsewhere, they go up 50%. And then the house that I don't expect to get sold sells right away. I am just amazed at how my surroundings don't make sense to me, how there is no logic to it. No rhyme or reason. Life is surely teaching me that it has more power than my thoughts. My actions do not necessarily dictate the path to the right future. It certainly makes me doubt my visions, and then I can't trust my gut feelings anymore because I think to myself, if the world happenings are in a way that I am astounded, then how can I supply proper information to myself upon which I am to make sound decisions? I even go as far as thinking to myself that if I am so out of touch with reality, how can I give the proper advice to my kids for choosing the right path for their lives and careers?

I think to myself maybe I have to get used to really strange happenings in the world around me. And then I think to myself, well then, if life is ruled by the law of randomness, then at times, these really shocking happenings would also be to my advantage. So, I am now looking to see how my path could cross with really shocking events that make my happy dreams come true. Even if I am not in control at all, and I am not good at making predictions about the path that life will take, there must still be some random events that come in my favor. They call this good luck or opportunities.

I must be ready to see these moments of good luck and opportunities and take advantage of them when they occur.

CHAPTER 37
AGAINST THE CROWD
8/5/2007

All my life, I have gone against the crowd. Even from my childhood, I remember the fad was to do something, but I would do something else. Soccer was the number one game where I grew up. I also played volleyball and track. And now, as I go into my grown-up life, people follow a fad, and I don't join in. Everybody bought stocks; I cried wolf and just watched when people were making big bucks. Then people bought real estate for investments; I said failure is on the horizon, and I kept watching people take advantage of the rising prices to get set for their retirement.

Every time I go against the crowd, I fall behind. They make the money, and I watch them from the sidelines. Why do I strive to be different? Do I think I'm actually smarter than everybody else? I don't think I'm smarter. If anything, I'm just as smart, so why don't I just do what everybody else does?

The book "Discover Your Destiny" says that it is just not good to follow the crowd, but you know what? I'm tired of trying to be special and then missing the boat. I want to catch the wave-like everybody else. Next time I see a wave, I'm going to catch it, and I'm going to ride it because I want to reach the high point in my financial life. I want to make it big like everybody else and ride the wave to the top of the world. I want to go with the flow. I don't want to feel and look different. I want to be part of the crowd. I want to grow with the crowd, and I want to prosper like everybody else. I can always change direction in the middle of the road and take off exponentially or sit back and enjoy my gains, but at the start, I follow what the crowd sees. Open your eyes and see what people see.

Take the risks early because you will still have time to correct your level of risk and direction and get it right. Make a move early, overcome your initial fears, and give power to your thoughts of success rather than calling doom every time you see something becoming popular.

CHAPTER 38
WHEN THE TIDE KEEPS GOING AGAINST YOU
10/21/2007

I started coaching this soccer team. It was probably going to be my last season coaching. I was looking forward to a fun season. I was not expecting much, but I promised I'd do my best to get the kids somewhere good. We started to play, and at every game, something kept going wrong. It soon started to seem to me that the referees had us marked to make calls against us to make us lose. One game, two games, three games, I said nothing and blamed it all on bad luck and kept reminding the kids that that's the way it is and playing on and acting as if nothing happened. I wouldn't let my nerves get distraught and would keep my calm and try to cool off my players, too, which was the right thing to do anyway.

By our sixth game, when things kept going unfairly wrong against us, I realized that if I let things go and allowed the tide to go against me, life and the world would continue to abuse me and crush me and take what rightly belongs to me away from me and treat me like nothing.

I decided that it was time to speak up and speak out. I could not let my kids get penalized for what they had not done. I could not see the laws being broken to put us at an unfair disadvantage. I had to speak out. I had to make them realize they could not walk over us. I had to show them we have dignity and respect for ourselves and that we value our rights. I started to point out the mistakes of the referee, made comments, and tried to engage them, albeit politely and with caution. It was scary and not my tradition, and it was uncomfortable, but when I realized that as a result of my speaking out, I may have already made them become better referees, I became more fearless. I was making my mark on life. I was changing the world in a good direction. I was making things look better. All of a sudden, I saw my team starting to live up to my expectations. I started to get results. My players were starting to feel proud of themselves because they saw somebody standing up for their rights.

It is not in my character to speak out when I see something going wrong or somebody doing me wrong, but now I realize that I am doing myself, the people who are under my care, and the world at large suffer in order for me to remain in my comfort zone. I need to challenge myself to let people hear what I have to say, and even if 90 percent of the time I may not be greeted with enthusiasm, I shouldn't care because the other 10 percent, when my voice makes a difference, I will be remembered for it.

Chapter 39
Everybody is Crying
2/4/2008

Recently, I noticed everybody was crying. Albeit for different reasons, at different times, and in different places, they find the time to cry, or at least they tell others that they are crying. One person is crying because they cannot afford to buy a multimillion-dollar home, another is crying because they cannot buy thousand-dollar gifts, while another is crying because they don't have the required $500 rent to keep a roof over their head. The younger keep crying about getting a grade D in a class or a test or not having gotten invited to a birthday party that everyone else was invited to. We are all crying. And it does not matter what is the reason that we are crying for. As long as we have something to cry for, we can cry and find the time to feel down enough to cry for it and waste our valuable minutes of life crying over what we don't have, should have, could have, or would want to have.

Somebody is crying because their team didn't win the Super Bowl, another is crying because he lost a lot of money betting on the Super Bowl, and a third is crying because he didn't win enough on the Super Bowl. I saw last night in my dreams that some guy was crying because he had lost his daughter, and I was crying because he had lost his daughter, and then while I was walking in the streets of downtown to buy a gold chain for my pendant, I saw a guy eating ice cream. At first look, I saw two prosthetic arms dangling by his side resting on the wall, and I started to think somebody was trying to fake something, but then I noticed that he was holding the ice cream cone with two arms that were amputated halfway up. Then I started to cry. He had probably cried a lot before, but he wasn't crying now. Maybe he cries at night when no one is looking.

This crying business is really amazing. We keep crying for the wrong reasons and for things that really don't matter, and we don't know what some other people are crying over. What seems so important and valuable to us may be so worthless to another.

When do we learn and pay attention to what really matters?

CHAPTER 40
LETTER TO A FRIEND, JULY 2, SOMETIME IN THE TWENTY-FIRST CENTURY

Today I found this letter that I wrote to a friend. From the color of the paper that had turned yellowish, I could tell it had been sitting in my drawer for a long time. It was never sent, but maybe one day, it will be read.

Dear Friend,

It is 4 o'clock in the morning on Sunday, and I can't sleep because of all the thoughts in my mind. I got up to write them down; maybe I'll send them to you someday.

Your email reminded me of my Mom's teachings. "Aim for the highest branch, and try your best to get there, but if you don't get there, be happy wherever you land."

Your writing and thoughts were pretty good. You said, "There isn't one single factor alone that can entirely account for a certain behavior. A degree in Psychology has taught me at least that much. As to what those various contributing factors may have been, it is unimportant to me. Regardless of what those factors may have been, in the end, I am still who I am. So instead of trying to find out why I did not win the lottery, I expend my energies in making the best life possible as a non-millionaire". My dear friend, what my Mom also taught me was to rise above my problems. Rise above my destiny. Don't just accept what is dealt to me in the game of life. Fight, persevere, and get back what should have rightly been yours. Get what you deserve.

Imagine where we would be or what the history of our family would have been if we had just accepted that we are not, as you put it (and I'm sure you are using this only as a euphemism) millionaires. Imagine how things would have been if we had not insisted on making any changes in our lives to better serve ourselves and our families first.

When I got a tumor in my neck, I could have said: well, I did everything right in my life by not drinking and smoking and living a healthy lifestyle, and if now I am destined to have a tumor, I'll accept it. I very vividly remember the thought that was most prominent in my mind: what will my children feel if I'm gone? What will my mother, brother, and others feel if I'm not there for them? They invested so much into me to someday reap the rewards of being part of my life and family. Is it fair for me to seek the easy way out? I had the surgery to remove my tumor (as any person in his right mind would have done), and to many doctors that completed my treatment. There was no sign of disease anywhere else. Should I have stopped there? This became the biggest challenge of my life because the road to security was a very difficult road, more difficult than I could ever come to believe. But I took it. I endured nine months of chemotherapy, as harsh as they come. What kept me going was that I deserve better than what this circumstance may bring upon me; my family deserves better than this, and I have to fight. I could have just accepted what was given to me. A few months or years of extra time and accept that it is okay if I won't be there for my child's Bar Mitzvah or wedding or to see a grandchild, okay that I won't be there to guide my children through life. But I opted not to take the easy way out even though I might have still been safe. I had to go beyond to make sure that I had taken every step to ensure that my life would continue as close to normal as I had expected it to be so that there would be no regrets later. I remember very vividly looking into my Mom's eyes when I was explaining to her that

I was going to go through chemotherapy, even though, in my heart, I really was scared and did not want to go through the tumultuous road of chemotherapy. She wanted me to live, to survive, and to have a full life. I had an obligation to her. I had an obligation to give her the chance to see many more happy moments of my life. As it turned out, the nine months of chemotherapy stole away nine valuable months of good times that I could have spent with Mom, and Mom didn't survive much more beyond my chemotherapy to enjoy all that we have longed for, and believe me, I spend many days thinking that I should not have done chemo so I wouldn't have wasted away those valuable last few months. But when I really came to terms with it, I did the right thing because that is what she wanted me to do, and that's what my children needed me to do. I could not be selfish and just think about what makes me happy or what is easy for me. The thoughts came back to me after every single round of chemo, and every time, after ten days of harsh treatment, I would contemplate quitting. But the thought of my family's expectations was the only thing that gave me the goal to go back and finish my treatment to become whole again. On this day that is Father's Day and the anniversary of Mom's passing, and also exactly five years to the day since the start of my treatment, I'm happy that I did what I did to buy me five years of life, not because I have particularly enjoyed my life, but because I know what my presence has meant to others…and I'd do it all over again if I had to although I know that it would morally and physically devastate me to go through chemo again.

Can you imagine where Mom would be if she had accepted her fate as it was put in front of her? The ninth child in a family of 11 and not much to be proud of being a girl in those days. All her brothers were succeeding in great endeavors, and her sisters were getting married in safety. She steered her life away from a life situation that was ruining her life and made something very valuable to a whole lot of people out of it.

Where would our friend be if he had accepted his fate when he was wrongly put in the prisons of Tehran after the revolution?

My dear friend, I know what you went and are going through (but I probably know half of your hardship the same way people can only imagine half of what I went through). It must be hard being between a rock and a hard place. But you have to realize all this is so that you may find your true self and not what life has imposed on you. You are such a flexible person. You are so well equipped to adjust yourself to whatever situation appears. But maybe you can be just as happy or possibly even more whole if you someday decide to change your path and try something different than your past few years. If that thought ever comes to your mind, embrace it and dwell on it in a positive way.

My dear friend, we are not on the other side of your life. We are you and your life. We are full of compassion and care. The care might not always seem to be in the direction you long for, but in every person's life; there are many times that they get influenced by their parents (or others who care just as much) in a direction other than they desire. What I want to emphasize most is that these discussions do not make you or me a bad person. We are still two of the best human beings that exist on the face of the earth. You have done a lot of good in your life, and I am confident that the future will bring a lot more good out of you for me, our family, and the world around us, no matter what. You have a good heart and a thoughtful, intelligent mind that we will always be proud of. Congratulations on having such high self-esteem to survive all this mess. I wished I could have some of your ability to handle the ordinaries of life in spite of all of its difficulties.

Love,

Your Friend, Now and forever

85

Chapter 41
Reflections on the Past, Steps to the Future
11/11/1999

Today, I took a major step in my life. A step to put behind my past and start a new beginning. I declared that I am not disabled from cancer anymore. Whether cancer ever comes back or whether I die prematurely from any other cause is not the point. The point is that I beat it at least once. The tumor that started to ruin my life three years ago has left me. I had a terrible battle, some of which I thought was unnecessary, but whatever I did, I did it to survive. And I have survived.

My last scans and MRIs show I'm clear. So now it is up to me to make the best of my life. Of whatever of it is left and of whatever of it is ahead of me. Remember my patient Louis, who, after Hodgkin's lymphoma and surviving it and after dropping near dead to a heart attack in the middle of nowhere in an airplane on a tarmac, came back against all odds, and then he wanted to have whiter teeth to look better. Well, the gift of life has been given to me, and it is up to me to make the best of it. To use it to my best advantage. And it is going to be a fight; it won't be easy. None of it was. But I have to declare war. And then I have to go go go till I get where I want to be, where it is good for me to be, where my family and I will be happy.

The main questions remain: Where do I want to be? What do I want to have? What do I want to get? What do I want to have done? What do I want to leave behind? What do I want to feel? How do I want to get there? What matters most? What does not matter? How happy do I want to be every day? What things should not make me unhappy? What things should I not do? What things must I do? How do I want my physical condition to be? How strong and healthy do I want to be in ten years?

So, with all these questions, it is now obvious that I need direction in my life. My huge Titanic has been pushed off the course by the forces of nature. All the bad and unwanted things that happened to me. They were not fair, and we didn't deserve them, but they did happen. Now, I am left with my wife, my two kids, brother, sister, nieces and nephews, in-laws, and friends. They are great people and have much to offer to me. I should use it.

So now that I am not disabled anymore, I have to devise a plan for success. A plan to do what I want to do and what I need to do.

CHAPTER 42
CHANGE IN PATH
5/18/2002

Twinkle, twinkle, little star, how I wonder what you could have become.

I wonder if, at a particular point in my life, some 15-20 years ago when I used to go to Redondo Beach bicycling, what and where would I have been now if I had made a different decision or sets of decisions in my life? Would I have still experienced the same events in my life in the same sequence, or would I have started down a whole new path with a new set of experiences and events, which could have been better or worse?

Am I willing to give up all my present-day experiences and exchange them for the unknown, new, and different experiences that might have been? If I have any doubt about giving up my "new experiences," then that truly can only mean that as bad as my life may have appeared at times, I am pleased and satisfied with the life I've had so far. If my life experiences were so worthless till now, then I would be able to give it up for a new set of experiences in the blink of an eye. But somehow, I see that things could have been worse. That I could have had less, felt less, been less, and meant less in other people's lives. And I am not willing to give those up. I still have a lot of good things, my wife and kids and family, with enough wealth and knowledge to prosper. I have to be thankful for all these and rejoice every day for having them. It is time that I quit thinking about what could have been and where I could have been. It is what it is, and the likelihood that I would still be in the same place with almost all the same experiences is great, and there would have been no change in my life experiences and status.

The plot of the movie life is all the same; just the actors and actresses would have been different with little change in any of the emotional states and factors.

Chapter 43
Renewal
11/20/2002

I made the move I had to. I sold our house and moved to a temporary rental home. I moved from the area where my kids were born and raised to an area where they will have better friendships and companions. Although scary at first, it led to new air, and I feel I am in a better spot, at least for the present time. And that is what counts, for the present to be good. I have worked hard all my life to make the future good, sacrificing the present for it. And then, when the future that was supposed to be rosy arrived, some bad event would ruin it. I have to make the present good. Now, this minute, today, right here, with who is here now. The present is where life takes place, not the past, not the future. I have to make the present be what I want, not sacrifice the present for the unknown future, and seize the moment.

In order to enjoy the moment and make the now the best, I have to stop worrying about the future. I can plan for the future and make things go in the direction I want but don't give up today by worrying about later. Take the worry out of your life by trusting the future will be the best that it can be, and the future will neither be better nor worse if you give up today for it. The future will be what it was going to be, what it has to be, what it wants to be. Only by taking advantage of life today can you store up on the goods so that you'll see the future with better eyes when it arrives.

Are there people in your life who are inhibiting you from loving and enjoying your moment-to-moment? Offer them your guidance and support their transition if they look up to you for it, but don't immerse yourself in their dilemma. Their problem is their problem. Don't worry about the whole world; you are neither God nor the king of any nation. You are an ordinary person only responsible for yourself, your family, and your immediate surroundings. Put your thoughts and energy where it counts, right here, right now.

Renew yourself, renew your energy, renew your lease on life, renew your attitude, renew your vision, renew your input into the life of others, renew your courage to face life, renew your stamina, renew your love of life. God has given you a soul; you are responsible to replenish it with joy and pleasure. It is your responsibility to feed it good stuff no matter how much bad arrives. The good always wins.

CHAPTER 44
WHAT'S LEFT
6/19/2003

I feel so helpless, resourceless, frustrated, demolished, and incapable. I decided to take one little step forward, one day at a time, as suggested to me in a book I was reading. It said that as long as one takes one short step every day, eventually, it results in a big move in the right direction. I see that I'm going nowhere. I work hard and struggle and try to do my best to make ends meet. To push things a millimeter forward. I get squished, I get up and walk, and then run again, continuing on my path. But I get nowhere. I'm still on the road after 45 years of concentrated effort, still closer to my starting point than to my goal. I don't know what else to do, and I don't have much more strength left in me to push the boulder of life forward. I know I expect too much of life. That despite having it better than a great majority, I feel I have nothing. I know that if I packed all of my luggage with my intelligence, ability, know-how, and possessions and set up camp somewhere new, I would still be in the top 10 percent of the population.

So why is it that I perceive myself as such a failure here?

I think it is because I measure things as a percent of change, not as base value, and as long as that percent of change is less than the percent of change I see around me, I feel like a failure and nothing has been accomplished. I care too much about this percentage of change. About where I was a few years ago and where I am now. I don't realize that with all that has happened, I could have easily been running into negative red, and just being able to maintain the status quo is a 100% improvement on what it could have been. I'm using the wrong yardstick to measure my progress and I have pictured an imaginary wrong baseline to calculate the percent change from. I should open my eyes and see what I have maintained. That by itself is a big deal.

Above all, be happy for what there is; it is not that bad, and there is a lot to treasure.

So now, as I am sitting on the porch overlooking Lake Tahoe and waiting for lunch after attending my seminar from work in this restaurant, I realize that life is not a bowl of cherries, and there are forces in the world that try their utmost to ruin the perfect present. You cannot control the forces nor change the evidence and the sour events left behind by those forces. However, you do have the choice to look away and not see what those forces left behind. You do have the choice to look the other way and take note of the little beauties that remain unaffected by the bad forces. It was a beautiful moment a few seconds ago sitting out here, but suddenly, the hard wind started to blow and ruined a perfectly good lunch. Good and bad were both present. I had the choice to dwell on the bad, or I could ignore it and concentrate on the little beauties around me.

In a couple of days, I will be going back home. Having been alone, I have now realized how much I have with my family. From this point on, I have not been allowed to see the world or life as a burden. Life is a beautiful garden that has been given to me. To enjoy it is my duty. To be happy in it is my God-given right. I must travel in this garden and plant new seeds to make it more beautiful, allowing for prettier flowers to grow. It doesn't mean that it is never going to rain or be dark in this garden; I have to see it as is and get past it, leaving it in the past where it belongs.

I am to enjoy the gift of having a good family and many friends. I have to take their love and give them love. I have to be there for them just as I expect them to be there for me. It is my duty to give them joy and happiness. It is my duty to let them live life fully. It is my duty to make them feel the world belongs to them. I have to promise myself not to let the ugliness around me take my chances of enjoying the perfect good away from me. It is up to me to dwell on the beauties. Expect bad luck and bad events and traumas, but don't dwell on them. They never go away; they are relentless, but you do have a choice to not let them ruin you. Don't get bogged down by them. Enjoy what is, to the utmost.

CHAPTER 45
PASSING THOUGHTS
8/1/2006

What is my purpose in life? What is the purpose of this life? Is it just to have fun and make the best of it until we come to a point of choice? The choice point is where we need to exercise our will, and that is where and when our purpose in life will become clear and evident and show us a crucial turning point. Maybe my purpose in life is not a perpetual thing. Maybe I have not even reached the point in my life when my being is necessary to exert a changing force, and all I have to do meanwhile is to have fun, take care of my family, and move on from day to day until I reach the day that destiny has set up for my purpose in life to become evident. So maybe I should stop searching for my purpose in life and instead should just live my life, and in time, my purpose will present itself to me. All I have to do now is enrich my life, learn, and gather tools in formation, stamina, and energy so that I'm prepared for the blastoff day.

Although I know how wrong it is, I am disappointed in life mainly because I do the work, and hence, I have some expectations for things to be a certain way, but yet when I look up and evaluate, almost nothing is going my way. It is frustrating to the self when the cycle of life seems to be out of tune with my being. When I appear not to be synchronized with life, I am dismayed. I want to be synchronized with life. I want to be in the same orbit, gaining energy from life and giving energy to life. I want happenings to go my way. I want to see things work out for me. Just like the magic of the dice in a game of backgammon when it gives you the great combination you need, I respectfully desire and want the roll of dice in the everyday events and happenings of my life to be in a way that makes me closer to my goals, wants, wishes, desires, and thoughts.

So, life, dear life, I beg you, let me be your friend and walk the walk of life along with you. I want satisfaction and happiness; I want things to go right for me. I want to be led in the direction that gets me closer to my purpose and destiny, freely choosing and doing what I desire to do along the way to bring me more happiness in my days, allowing me to gain greater respect for myself. Then when the choice point of my life presents itself to me and my purpose becomes clear to me, I can courageously take the necessary steps to make the difference I have to make in the world and in my life.

CHAPTER 46
LIFE MAKES YOU BIGGER
9/23/2006

I always wondered why people go through hardships. Why does life present us with challenges that seem to break us down and destroy us, often leaving us disheartened about life itself? People say there is always a lesson to be learned from every hardship, and everything happens for a reason, to make you stronger and feel more worthy, but I never believed that until today.

A few months ago, I had gone to my office, and it seemed to be another ordinary day at work. My receptionist was calling patients who had not been in for a while. She was on the phone with this lady, and I overheard that she couldn't come in for a while because she was sick. She was a very sweet lady, and I had known her for years, so I decided to get on the phone myself and talk to her.

She explained that she had been diagnosed with some form of cancer and she was going through a difficult time. I realized I had gone through many of those stages that she was explaining to me when I was sick, so I started to comfort her and explain to her that she was not the only person feeling that way and it is normal to go through all of those stages while under treatment, and I provided her with some of the advice and knowledge that I had gained from my experience through the years. We had a nice chat; I acknowledged her feelings and experiences and hung up the phone, thinking that I had done nothing helpful.

A month went by, and today, that lady came to my office for treatment. As she walked in, she came towards me and gave me a big hug. She went on to say how the ten-minute chat I had with her had changed her whole attitude towards her disease and her experiences and how she had been able to continue her treatment more easily and to completion because of the suggestions I had made to her. She was so thankful that it made me feel very proud of myself. Suddenly, I noticed that the ten minutes I had spent had not gone to waste, and it had actually made a big difference for someone. I felt good that I had opened my mouth and shared my emotions fee, feelings, and experiences. But more importantly, I learned a valuable lesson. I realized that the horrible experience that I had gone through had made it possible for me to make life easier for at least this one person. She had a better life because of me. I had found value and purpose in my life and living. I realized that my existence was now important because it could change the course of someone else's life. My experience had made me a bigger person than I was. They say the purpose of life is to turn you into a mountain, not into a piece of dirt. And surely, I was getting closer to feeling like a mountain now.

CHAPTER 47
WAITING TAKES LONGER
10/11/2006

Have you ever noticed how long it takes for that red traffic light to turn green? And no matter which direction you travel in at a specific intersection, your red light takes longer while you are waiting. When you enter a doctor's office, you keep waiting impatiently for the staff to open the door and call your name, and it takes so long, longer every time as you wait. When you are waiting for the taxi or your ride to arrive, how long it takes while you are waiting, all ready to go, and getting impatient every minute that goes by and they have not arrived yet, and your wait seems to get longer and longer.

But the other day, I noticed something different though. I was driving, I heard an advertisement on the radio, and I wanted to write down the phone number. As I reached a red light for the first time, I would be happy that I was hitting a red light so I could write the number down. But as soon as I would take the pen to write, the light would turn green. After this happened a few times, I became suspicious, and I wondered if there was a conspiracy so I would forget the phone number or if somebody was trying to get me to lose my green light. But when I started to time the red light, I realized that it was the same as I had measured it on my watch on other days.

I started to pay attention. It seemed to me whenever I was waiting for something to happen, it was taking longer. Somehow, it seemed that waiting and paying attention to waiting would make the wait appear longer. But when I would put my attention on something else, time would fly by a lot faster. I honestly timed a red light once, and it took 17 seconds to get green. Then, every day, as I would get stuck behind the same light, I would start counting down. It seemed the seconds were taking longer each day. But then I started to sing the song on the radio instead of counting the seconds, and before I could sing a single line, the light would turn green, and I would have to take off.

Our moments in life are valuable. So valuable that it is a waste to spend it waiting for anything. Never wait. Also, make it so that time has to chase you. Always keep so busy that you are asking for time to travel more slowly than to keep wishing that time would go by faster.

CHAPTER 48
WINNING IT FAIR AND SQUARE
12/25/2006

It was the end of soccer season for the team that I was coaching. We had come a long way. We started off the season as a team that had little chance of any win in the beginning, especially after the people who were in charge of the distribution of the top players decided that I was too strong of a team despite our loss in the first game and removed my top player and traded him for a weak player. We had worked our way up the ladder, and we had enough wins to go to the playoffs. I was working really hard on my team to create cohesiveness and make the team play in unison, and it worked out well. We somehow made it to the championship game, winning it fairly and squarely without any apparent lucky breaks or events. The teams just played well, and both teams had an equal chance of winning at the start. It didn't seem to me that anyone was getting any special treatment.

The championship game was a hard-fought game, and it seemed to me I was finally poised to have had a team that would get the championship medal. When the second half started, I noticed some calls by the referee that were going against us and did not seem correct to me. But, being one who always wants to put trust and respect in the higher authority, and not wanting to be confrontational, and also respecting the game, I said nothing and did nothing. I knew some of the kids on the other team had parents in the organization, and I was starting to form a doubt in my mind as to whether anything was going on that I didn't know about. After another seemingly bad call, my assistant blew off the top and started yelling, but again, I tried to calm him down to our own disadvantage, and I told him I wanted to win the game fairly and squarely.

We lost the game by virtue of calls that were not fair and square. I wondered to myself, which is more noble, to let go of apparent actions that put me at a disadvantage just to show that I am a man of integrity, albeit at the expense of those under my wings having an unfair result, or to try to use any physical and psychological opportunity to turn the wave of events to benefit me or my team. I questioned whether doing this should depend at all on whether I am the beneficiary of the outcome or if people under my care are the actual recipients of my actions. Does it matter whether my trying to gain an unfair advantage has any dependency on my selfishness or altruism? Should I feel that if I am fighting for someone else's rights, I should use any crack to my advantage to win the game, whether it is a game of soccer or another game in life? I realized that it is done all over the place by everyone to win their right, whether it is a fight in the Supreme Court or just a game of cards. People always want to be winners, and they don't look at what the means is. If they can delay the start of a game so the other team gets tired or frustrated waiting on the field or create havoc so it mentally reduces the opponent's ability to perform, almost all human beings look out for their own good and don't pay attention to the Karma, and think that just winning that one time is and should be their highest goal, irrespective of what effect it will have on someone right then and there, or in the following years, or on future generations. I was kind of disappointed that in all the years of schooling, no system was actually in place to teach and educate our kids about how to play it fair and square, and how my learned behavior of playing it fair and square for whatever reason I was feeling propelled to, was working to my disadvantage and at a cost to those whose happiness and wellbeing depended on my actions. I also realized that winning it fairly and squarely does not mean sitting still and letting life happen. You have to take action and show that you care and you know, even if it means that you will show others that your actions are fair and square and that you are, in addition to honoring your cause, standing for fairness, not only for the sake of your own peace of mind but also to show that you care for those who can't stand up for themselves.

Do I need to rethink this whole fair and square idea? Is there a higher purpose than getting what you just want for today? Maybe time will tell, and my journey into life will give me a clearer picture.

CHAPTER 49
THE FEAR EXPERIENCE
1/1/2007

On this particular Sunday, I needed to pick up some stuff from the Hardware store. I spent an hour in there picking everything I needed. Some big items and many small pieces that took me some time to figure out and find. As I approached the cashier's stand, I noticed the light bulb section. I parked my cart in front of the aisle and went to find the bulb I needed. After about 10 minutes, I found what I needed and went to my shopping cart. I couldn't find it where I last left it. At first, I thought another customer may have taken it by mistake, so I started to look around to see if there were any unattended shopping carts around or if there was any sight of my own cart. None.

I went to one of the Red Jacket customer service persons nearby, and I explained. He said they probably took it away to return and re-stock the items. He said to go check with the "Returns section." I went, and from afar, I saw a couple of my items on a cart. I explained to the person what had happened, and she graciously let me inside to go and check. To my dismay, many items were already dispersed. I had spent so much time picking that stuff up. How could they do this to me? I called the manager and complained, and he said that it was store policy and they didn't do anything wrong. He even asked me to get out of the area and not continue to look for my items there. I was frustrated and left the store.

Several weeks later, I needed to get some other stuff from the same place. As I entered, I could see the Red Jacketed customer service personnel roaming around. I immediately felt threatened, and the sight of the previous time's unpleasant experience flashed in front of my eyes. I picked up some stuff that I needed. I noticed I needed something from the aisle next door. I left my cart there and went to the other aisle. As I was searching on the shelves, suddenly, the feeling of fear from what had happened the previous time came over me, and I started to get nervous. Hurriedly, I went back over, and luckily, I gave a sigh of relief as I saw my cart was still there. I started to walk along and soon passed by one of the Red Jacket people. I could feel my heart rate go up again. I started to think how terrible it was that even after such a trivial, unimportant unpleasant experience, I could experience such anxiety. I could almost feel for people who have had a bad traumatic experience and how it would affect them. Also, imagine how some who have been exposed to repeated traumas, like being in a war, would have such lingering feelings and how important it is to deal with them in a knowledgeable cognitive way.

I had to sit with myself for a while and meditate and process the event and the feeling in order to clarify for myself that that was an isolated instance and that if something happens once, it does not mean it will happen again.

CHAPTER 50
THE LIVES THAT I AM LIVING
1/2/2008,

I hear all this talk about past lives and how we have all lived past lives and experienced different lives. Then I start to think whether it is possible that we are living different lives concurrently. Is it possible that our souls from our past lives have split up into different bodies, and we are experiencing different lives at the same time?

So, I start to think, if I am looking at somebody and decide I like their life and what they are doing, could it be that I am already experiencing that life? What if the soul in that body is already my soul, and I am already living it? Wouldn't that take away all jealousy? If I can have whatever I want, and by I, I don't mean my bodily physical I, I mean my I soul, then isn't it great when I realize and recognize that I am already doing what I yearn for and what I like just because my soul is already living it. Depression is brought about by a lack of control over what you want life to be. When life takes control of you, and you can't make things happen the way you had imagined, then you lose hope, and you start to feel helpless and down. But how about if you suddenly remember that even if your life is not what you have wanted and imagined, then all of a sudden, you may see somebody living the life you have wanted and looked for? All you have to imagine is that your soul is part of that experience, and although your physicality is not participating in the events, maybe your soul and memory are.

Sometimes, we unexpectedly know things that there is no reason we should know because we have never experienced them. But somehow, there is a gut feeling that exists within us, and we know how a certain experience is going to shape up based on our past experience. But when we search our past experiences, we don't see any time that we experienced such a thing. Yet we have a strong feeling about it. Could it be that our soul that had parted from our main soul drifted into some other body and experienced some event and now has reunited with its parted soul in this lifetime, and therefore, this soul in this lifetime has knowledge of that certain event and experience, and the memory exists in the soul, even though the body has not experienced it? Is it possible that when a child is so good at music, math, or playing soccer, it is because part of their soul in a previous life lived the life of a musician, mathematician, or soccer player?

So now that I am living this life, I think to myself: how did all those previous lives build up what I am today, and how it is going to shape my future and the future of all those different bodies that it is either occupying now or will occupy in the future. Does this mean that one has to treat everyone else with kindness and a good heart because they may be giving that treatment to their own soul, and they will eventually be the recipient of what seed they plant?

Are we all one?

CHAPTER 51
DOES IT MATTER?
7/10/2008

I was coming back home after I spent a couple of hours in the temple. It was the anniversary of my mother's passing. I was in a somber mood. That night was going to be my niece's wedding. And today, I was being reminded of the greatness and loss of my mother. I was deep in my thoughts, strolling to my car. As I was going past the security guard, he looked at me and said:" Nice tie." I thought to myself, who cares? What does it matter? My mother is not here, and I miss her, and you are telling me I am wearing a nice tie? Or maybe it was his job to tell passersby good things to make them happy. I was wondering whether this could have been a message from up there, telling me to wake up and celebrate; the time for mourning is over. Look at the beauty in things instead of your loss. This guy's comment was totally unexpected. Nobody ever compliments me on the things I wear, and now a stranger compliments me on my tie on a hot summer day when I am not in the mood to talk to anyone.

I thought to myself, does it matter that this guy said something, and does it matter if I actually am wearing a nice tie? There are so many other very important things in my life that I am concerned with right now, and whether my tie is nice or not is totally irrelevant. What is the purpose of this comment?

After a few steps, I thought to myself that, at the least, this guy's comment was a nice, polite gesture, and at the greatest length, it was a Godly message that there is still some beauty in the world even though everything around us looks like it is falling apart. He was telling me that despite all the bad people

I had come across that week, there were still good people around. There is a world that I can trust and feel good about. Even one person, one word, one comment, and one smile can make a difference.

CHAPTER 52
WHERE IS SHE?
9/11/2008

My Mom passed away 11 years ago. I remember the moment I arrived at her condo and saw her lifeless body on the carpet; something compelled me to go over, put my hand over her shoulders, and recite the "Shema," as I had been told is proper to do upon one's death. Till today, I still wonder why there is no sign of her around. I don't mean that physically I expect her to be here, but you know how they say when someone is gone, they still give signs and make events happen, making you think that they are still hanging around and taking care of issues. Well, a lot of times, I start to talk to my Mom and ask her where she is, where she went, and what happened. She loved family so much that I always thought that even when she left us in body, she would still be around in spirit. But haven't really gotten a feel for that, and I wonder to myself, is it because we did something wrong and she was trying to get away from us, or did she have something better to do than hang around with us, just like when I was little, and there were tons of things she had to do for the community instead of being around me.

This has actually made me feel guilty a lot of times, thinking to myself that maybe there is something I should do or there is something that I should have done, like saying the Kaddish a million more times or writing about her a hundred more pages or given to charity in her name more often. Maybe I messed up somewhere along the line, and that made her soul run away from us.

Then, all of a sudden, I remembered that maybe it was not something bad that I did. It is the Shema that I recited when she passed away. Maybe by virtue of the Shema that I said, I freed her soul to go where it needed to go, to a new world and new life and new experience, rather than be bound here in life and hanging around with us. Maybe I am the one who gave her wings and freedom, and nobody is to blame for her not being around, and actually, her not being around is a good sign, meaning going one step higher to Nirvana.

Instead of blame, I now feel that I have fulfilled my duty. I did what a righteous son was supposed to do to allow the soul of his mother to gain the freedom it needed to travel closer to God. I needed to let go. I need not feel guilty or accept blame for her not being present in our lives anymore, although we miss it tremendously.

CHAPTER 53
THIS WILL BE THE BEST YEAR OF YOUR LIFE
9/21/2008

It was January of 1996. I was reflecting on the events of the previous night, the New Year's Eve party at our house. It was such a wonderful night. We had planned to throw a party just the week before with no preparation. We invited our friends while we were driving up to Mammoth for a few days of skiing, and when we would come back, we would only have two days before the party to organize everything. But somehow, everything worked out well. Even the weather cooperated with us. Can you believe it? It's New Year's Eve, and it is 70 degrees outside with a little bit of a warm breeze that makes the air feel fresh and dry.

The party turned out to be a blast; everybody had so much fun. It was a really happy event. I was really excited and was thinking to myself that this was a good beginning to a new year, especially since we had suffered from some effects of the recession in the previous years. I was hoping that this would be the beginning of an economic boom for me and my family.

Anyway, the days of the new year started to go by, and I was still energized from my party. A few days later, I went to lunch at work. I went to a Chinese restaurant on 11th Street in Santa Monica. After the meal, I got a fortune cookie as usual and thought to myself that there was going to be a really good message in there for me.

I opened the cookie and was amazed at what the fortune read: "This year will be the best year of your life." I was astounded. First, the amazing blissful events of the previous days made me feel that I was on the top of the mountain of happiness, and everything was going so well for me at work and home now. This fortune is telling me that the rest of it is going to be the best. Wow. I put the fortune paper on the dashboard of my car so I would see it every day. It was a reminder to me that every day is a good day. I was getting myself ready to experience the best year of my life.

Who knew, though, what events were in store for me? Till March, life was great, and I was riding the wave of joy. On the last day of March, suddenly, all hell broke loose when my mother had a car accident and broke both her legs. It was a disaster. So sad. Why such a calamity for her at this stage of her life? Thanks to God, she survived the accident, but nonetheless, the pain and suffering were great. Alas, we managed to get by, and as the days went by, she was healing another bad news. After a series of unknown events, I found out I had a cancerous tumor in my neck and had to have an operation. Not bad, I thought to myself. I'll have the operation immediately and start my road to healing quickly. I know I have a strong body, and I will recover from it quickly. And, of course, time was very crucial. My mother needed help to quickly heal and improve her condition, and my niece's wedding was coming up in June. On June 13, I had the surgery, and in 2 days, I was out of the hospital, thanks to God and good surgeons, and on my way to a quick recovery. Actually unbelievable. I healed so quickly and so well that I was dancing full blast at my niece's wedding, a very happy occasion in many ways, although there were some bittersweet moments mingled in since my Mom was still confined to a wheelchair and couldn't join us on the dance floor. The day after the wedding, I was to see this specialist familiar with my rare form of tumor. He recommended chemotherapy and made it seem a very easy process and a very necessary thing to do. I, adamant about making this the best year of my life and longing to experience it fully, accepted it right away and started treatment on July 2.

It didn't take me long to find out that the treatment that this doctor had recommended for the following nine months would be a trip to hell. The chemo was very intense, and I got really sick from it every time. But somehow, the will to live for the benefit of my kids and family outweighed any pain I was experiencing.

Sometime during the process, I remembered the fortune cookie and what it said. This is going to be the best year of your life. What did that mean now, I wondered. The meaning was not clear to me anymore. If that were to be true, why all the sour events? Why all the hardships? Am I going to make it through the year? Is that what it meant? That was the last year of my life, and hence, it could be, in a way, the best year of my life because it was leased time from God lent to me for a few months. December came, and another New Year, and my treatment didn't finish on time because I got sick with the flu, and they had to delay some of the treatments. And then they told me I had to have radiation therapy and I should be done by March of 1997. I was done, and still no sign of it being the best year of my life. By then, it was also clear to me that it wasn't my last. I had survived to another year, a blessing all by itself. By now, I was kind of belligerent towards the message in the fortune cookie. What sort of best is this, and did that fortune cookie wake up the evil eye?

I found the little piece of paper and tore it into pieces, knowing that certainly this past year could not have been the best year of my life. And then, on July 2, 1997, exactly one year from the day I had started my chemo, my mother died of sudden death. How could this be? She had healed so well, and she was in such good health and spirit. One bad year after another. These two definitely didn't qualify as the best years of my life. Not even close. I tried to convince myself that maybe the fortune meant it was the best because it was the last with my Mom, but then I knew how much pain and suffering she must have gone through while I was under treatment, and this certainly didn't feel like the best year. Life went by, and for about the next ten years, I resented what the fortune cookie had said.

Tonight was my 50th birthday, and I went to a Chinese restaurant to celebrate. When I got a fortune cookie, I was reminded of all the events, but something clicked differently. Maybe what the fortune was trying to tell me was that "This NEW YEAR start will be the best NEW YEAR start of your life," in which case the fortune would be totally on the mark since no New Year ever since has been as good. Indeed, that year was the best New Year of my life. I take it as a gift that was given to me and cannot be taken away, even with all the calamities that have taken place since. Any day that is the best ever is worth it all on its own merit and cannot be taken away and must be kept as a precious gift that was given to us. Just because it was one more good day in our life.

CHAPTER 54
WHAT IF GOD WORKED A SEVENTH DAY
10/11/2008

Dear God, forgive me. Everybody says and is proud that God worked six days and created heaven and earth and everything else in six days. And then, on the seventh day, he rested. And then they use this to create a day of resting for themselves, saying that if God took the seventh day off, we should too. They come up with all kinds of reasons and logic that would justify having a day off. Not that I am against having a day off. It is a wonderful idea, a time to rest and gain strength, to reflect on your life and actions, to catch up with life and all that you have to do, to be with yourself and your family.

Taking the seventh day off definitely has its health benefits and good reasons. But did God really need to take the seventh day off? He is, after all, the Almighty and tireless God that has for millions of years been guiding humanity gra, noting his wishes, and paving his way to more in this world. He is the superpower and, as such, probably could still function at full pace and activity. But now I ask myself, what if he had continued to work that seventh day to complete the world in a more perfect way? Can you imagine a perfect world where there wouldn't be pain, suffering, diseases, or tooth decay (oh, what a painful thing)? There wouldn't be bad deeds, hurricanes, earthquakes, global warming, etc. Could it be that by keeping working an extra day, he could have refined his creations a bit more so that for years to come and generations, he could have enjoyed a better fruit from his creations? Actually, I think what happened was because he took that one day off, and the earth and heavens had already been created and were rolling at an enormous speed, he fell behind, and till this day, he has been playing catch up to try to refine his creation and he can't because as soon as he fixes one thing the rolling speed of events have caused another mess and it keeps going on and on. It is just like the financial crisis of 2008, where things started to go bad so fast that no matter how much the Feds and the world leaders tried to harness the problem, it kept moving on at its own pace and out of control.

Likewise, maybe instead of having to fix things as they are going wrong every day, the Almighty should stop for a moment and see what is missing and what he should have and could have created in that seventh day that is the missing piece of the puzzle in his creation. Maybe if he had completed his creation as he should have done in the first place, he wouldn't have had to work so hard to keep fixing things now. Like fixing the people, what goes on in their heads, the actions, and the events that take place globally and in the universe every day, can you imagine what it would be like if no stars would implode? How many more stars would we have had in the sky, and how much more beautiful would the sky look?

But then maybe God knew all of this and yet decided to leave the world in an imperfect condition so that there is room for free will and chances of randomness. Maybe he knew that it is better to leave a little imperfection behind and take a day off to look back at your creation and rest and have time to give gratitude for what you have been able to do and to thank the universe for giving us the ability to cause creation. Maybe we best understand that we are not living in a perfect world, and we do not need to create perfectionism in our life, so long as we spend the majority of our time creating, building, and producing, and then take a little time to enjoy life and look inside, even if it means letting things go a bit wrong at times.

CHAPTER 55
SURPRISE
1/10/2009

For so long, I had been trying to get my son to be the best at doing something. I thought because I was good at sports, maybe he could become good at sports, also. So, since he was little, I tried to introduce him to all kinds of sports. I got him into soccer since it was my passion, hoping that it would also become his passion. I was good at soccer, so I thought he would become good at it, too. Over the years, we had many soccer teams and events. I kept coaching him and our teams and worked hard at teaching him and pushing him to become a good soccer player. But it never seemed to happen. There were always the others who seemed to do better. I eventually thought to myself well, I did what I could, and he is what he is. He is good enough, and that is good enough for me, and he will have lots of fun with his level of play.

We kept going to soccer events, and he continued with his high school team. A team that was generally not doing well. He had a certain attitude, and that was to get everybody excited and up and motivated. What he may have lacked in soccer skills, he made up in voice and friendship with his teammates. He always put his heart into it and gave it his best in a positive way. Things appeared to go in a routine, monotonous way. Until.............

One day, he came home and said that the coach was tired of all the infighting in the team. He gave a speech at the beginning of their game that day and fired all of the four current captains of the team since none of them were effective and everybody in the team was fighting them. He said he was looking for somebody who could lead the team and could make the team work together. He wanted the captain to be a coach on the field and be good in a way that everybody respected and would cooperate with him. Then, the coach turned to my son and said, "You will be the new captain of this team." Of course, my son's heart dropped at first, but then he realized that is what he was made to be: an organizer and a leader for the team. The coach spoke some more, and the game started. They won their first game. Hooray. Things are now happening that show me that all that hard work and coaching I did and showing him the way to lead did not go to waste.

I realized that all those years that I was coaching him in soccer, even though my goal was to improve his soccer skills, I was teaching something a lot more valuable: how to lead, manage, motivate, inspire, create coherence and success in the team. I hope that he will have many good years of success, knowing that even if you lose a game, you won't lose the lesson. Learn and move on, and in the end, your day of success will come.

CHAPTER 56
FREE WILL
2/14/2009

I propose a question. If we knew that when we enter this world, it would be for a single reason and find out that we could only behold and experience/observe that reason only once and perhaps a single moment, would we still choose to be born to experience that one thing, or would we choose to remain in a life of eternity without it forever.

So now I think to myself, what was the one thing that made me want to be reborn into this world and to choose it over a life of eternity? Of course, the usual thing of loving and being loved and feeling and tasting and experiencing life in living a lifetime is there, but what supremely immeasurable desire was the tipping point that made me leave eternal beingness and be born. Because if I find that reason, then that could by itself be my life purpose.

A life purpose doesn't have to be doing something for someone else or achieving something, I recently found. That is only the altruistic point of view. A more personal point of view could be that a life purpose is simply to experience something noble, unique, and worthy, something that has the capacity to change the way one sees the world or feels about eternity, the universe, and the almighty. And then we wait a lifetime to experience that one thing, even if it is for a moment, and then we are a fragile human being again till we meet our destiny of death.

So, if we arrived here by free will and we have either already come across that moment in our life that we gave up eternity for, or that moment is still waiting on the horizon and we just have to pass the time till we get there, then why not live our days enjoying the fruits of this world every day. We might as well taste every rightful joy and pleasure possible and allowed for us in this earthly world. We might as well live a playful life because when we meet the moment of our destiny that fulfills our life purpose, whether it is when we feel and touch our life purpose or whether it is when death has arrived upon us, we have smiled and created laughter and happiness, both for ourselves and others around us. Spend every moment of your life as if it were a gift, and you are here to experience it because, in the blink of an eye, it may be the end. You may not have the chance to touch her ever again, kiss her lips one more time, or smell her hair ever again. It is not that life has meant anything bad for you, and it definitely does not mean it is punishing you. It is just the way things are; you should know better.

So now that I am at this realization, my question is: "For what moment in life did I give it all up?". I know I made the jump so that I could feel that one thing, the moment in life that I so craved. What was it, or what is it? I feel I may have had that one moment in life that was in my supreme desire, and now I have to live and love every day of the rest of my life, and maybe there are more of those profound moments in store.

Chapter 57
Chance of occurrence
4/19/2009

I was playing backgammon with my friend. I lost to him 11 times in a row. Even though there seemed to be times that I was clearly in a position to win, close to the end, the roll of the dice would be such that it would give him an opportunity to hit one of my pieces, and sure enough, he would roll the dice that he needed to hit that one piece and win.

On the one hand, I can understand how he would roll the dice in a way that would allow him to get what he needed. That, of course, has to do with the power of intention. He intends something for himself, and he gets it. But what amazes me is how he and his intention can affect my toss. How does he manage to get the role that he wants out of my doing? Additionally, how is it that my intention of not getting the number that favors him and concentrating on the number that I do actually want does not materialize? Is it a constant battle between the two intentions? What is so strong about his intention that seemingly overpowers mine? Granted that he is a better player, and I don't mind losing to him because he truly plays well and with few if any, mistakes, but I also notice that when he takes a risk and exposes himself, he gets the subsequent roll that is necessary to make his plan complete. Is he actually reading into the future, or is he trusting the world and taking steps, knowing that things will turn for the better no matter what choice he makes? I don't believe that destiny has any part in this. Whatever it is, it must be an instantaneous burst of power and control that results in the acquisition of the desired result. How is this control manifested? Is it in the strength of the thought and power of the mind, or is it the transference of energy through the fingertips?

I bring up the fingertips because I also notice that I have several ways that I toss the dice. I think that is the root source of the problem. Because I keep switching patterns of movement, am I actually disturbing the flow of energy and disrupting the path of achievement? By the way, why don't the dice feel comfortable in my hands? When I am moving them around in the palm of my hand, sometimes it feels like I am stumbling when I actually release the dice. Do the dice realize this stumble, or rather, it is the flow of energy that is disrupted in this stumble? I've also noticed that if on a particular day, I have experienced misfortunes during the day, either at work or home, the dice pick up on that even more and generate even more antagonism. My attitude at the moment of the game gives direction to the statistical outcome.

I question whether fearfulness has any part in this development of results. Could it be that my friend has no fear of the outcome of the role that he rolls with such confidence that he gets what he wants? His positive thinking, energy, and vibration transmit direction to the game. If there is emotional duress, will that affect the transmittance of good vibes, not only to people but also to objects, no matter what the task at hand is?

CHAPTER 58
THE ORCHIDS THAT DIDN'T BLOOM
5/24/2009

About two years ago, I went to the orchid show in Santa Barbara. It was an amazing sight, acres of colorful orchids lined up to be sold to the public. It looked like a good year. It was March, a warm and sunny March. I went from one nursery to another, and I witnessed yet more amazing varieties of orchids. I had my big SUV with me, so I bought a number of plants and brought them home with me. I asked the sellers if these orchids give flowers every year. They gave me a combination of plant foods and told me to use these, and I would get good flowers every year. I will never forget how excited my wife was when I came home and my wife saw the car full of those colorful and unique plants. After a month of beautiful flowers, they disappeared, leaving the green leaves. I watered them on time, mixing in the plant food as was directed month after month, waiting impatiently for the flowers to reappear the following year and make my home beautiful and lively.

The following March arrived. It was a cooler year with not as much sun. No flowers appeared. None of the plants showed any sign of bloom. I thought maybe I did something wrong. So, the following year, I was very careful to follow instructions and do the feeding correctly. March arrived. I saw two of the plants had bloomed. They were beautiful flowers. I was ecstatic. Soon, I will have a yard full of pretty orchids, I told myself. I kept watering and feeding as per instructions, keeping my hopes high. But nothing more. About ten of the plants never bloomed. No sign of pretty flowers. April came and went by, and still nothing. I knew I had done everything right, but yet no result.

I realized that sometimes, no matter how hard you work and how good a job you do, some things will still not happen as if they have a mind of their own. So now I have a choice: dwell over the fact that they didn't bloom and keep blaming myself or others and living in dismay, or I can keep watering and feeding the plants, hoping that someday the flowers will come back. Life has a calendar of its own, and no matter how you force it to change, it will not because there is a bigger purpose in the grand scheme of events. We cannot understand why the flowers did not bloom, and I may take the plants to be researched as to why they didn't bloom, but the bottom line will not change. They just did not want to bloom.

Maybe my luck will change, and all of a sudden, all the plants will bloom just because it is the right time for them to bloom.

Fast forward to 3 years later, during which time I have given little attention to the nonflowering orchids and have given up hope that they ever will bloom. Suddenly, it is February, and I notice that all the orchids are blooming with the most gorgeous flowers. I am amazed. I did little, but I am getting results. Is it just because it is time?

CHAPTER 59
THE EMPTINESS OF THE FULL DVD'S
5/24/2009

I was watching TV, and suddenly, I took a glimpse at the stack of DVDs that were sitting on top of the TV. For weeks now, I have been converting my old videos to DVDs. All the VHS videos of my children's childhoods, when they were born, all the cute things they did, all the funny words they said, even further than that, going back to when I was a child myself. All the pictures and sounds had been transferred to the DVDs. Hour after hour of images, both still and moving. But when I looked at this stack of DVDs, I could see right through them. I could even see the silhouette of the objects behind them. It was the strangest feeling; all those images meant nothing. Even though the DVDs contained so much information on them, it all meant nothing; it was all nothingness. The images, sounds, and words occupy no space in our universe. All the memories were a pile of see-through objects. How could this be? When I put any of these DVDs in a player, I see hours of images, ones that are so powerful to bring laughter, tears, strength, weaknesses, emotions, and thoughts. But now they all sit on top of each other piled high, and even all of them together are still a stack of nothingness to my eyes.

Maybe it is because our memories and what happened in the past were dreams. Just like when we wake up in the morning and there is no physical evidence of our dreams or our past, even if it was all captured on video, it has no tangible matter to it. It could all have just as well been a dream.

CHAPTER 60
DOES IT MATTER?
6/11/2009

Recently, I was on my way to the airport to go overseas for a seminar. Since my plane was scheduled to leave in the early afternoon, I decided to skip going to work that day and stay home and take care of a few important things, including my loan application and process. During the morning hours, I got things done in a very organized fashion and also had enough time to go for a relaxing walk in the neighborhood. I told myself that in order to be at the airport in time for the international flight, I needed to leave home at noon. So around 11:55, I am having a light lunch from some leftovers from the previous night, and everything is going according to plan. All of a sudden, the phone rings, and it is my broker on the other end asking a few important questions about my loan application. Since I was leaving town, I had to get things done before I would leave, so I had to stay on the phone for 10-15 minutes to get all the necessary things done. Suddenly, I looked at my watch, and now I was 15 minutes behind schedule. I jumped and put things in my car in a hurry and started to go to the airport. The first route of travel hit major traffic, and I told myself I wouldn't make it in time if traffic continued that way all the way to the airport. So, I switched routes and took another road to a different freeway to the airport. Traffic was still heavy as it happened to be one of those middays when everybody was out shopping. I came across a yellow light turning red, and I tried to zoom through it, barely missing the red. I was thankful that the intersection did not have a camera; otherwise, I would have gotten one of those big fat tickets. But still, I continued the trek, being in a great hurry and swerving through the cars on the road to get to the airport faster.

I got there, checked my luggage, and went through security. All of a sudden, I noticed that I had a lot of time on my hands. I said to myself, does it matter that I hurried so much to get here? Does it matter what route I took? Does it matter that I was a little late or early? Does everything in life matter? Does everything that happens during the course of our lives make a difference in the end result? Does it matter what we eat, drink, and do on an hourly basis, or is there a major destiny that awaits us no matter what little things in between we decide to do?

CHAPTER 61
IS IT A BAD DAY?
6/30/2009

The day had started with a somber mood. I had been waiting seven years for an opportunity to buy a house in the location that I wanted with the kind of things in it that I wanted, and as the days went by, it seemed I was getting further away from my dream becoming reality. I had finally come across this house that seemed to have most of the requirements that I had, and the price, although high, was affordable. It was an expensive house, and by anyone's standard, it would be a lavish expenditure. If anyone has had any experience buying a house, you know that there are always many glitches that come up along the way. My experience was no exception, and in the past four weeks that I had been in the escrow and purchasing process, many issues that, at times, were letdowns had come up. But each time, and usually by giving in and becoming flexible towards what I wanted, I would make the process move along. But today, it seemed to be the end of the line. We needed and had applied for this big loan, and the broker had previously told me that I would be getting the loan, so the path to purchase seemed clear, but all of a sudden, two days ago, the broker called saying the bank could not approve the loan yet and it has to go through a special committee, and it would take ten more days to hear the results. However, the deadline for the loan contingency was three days, so we called the seller to ask for an extension. But today, my broker called me and said that the seller was not willing to give any further extensions and that we would have to cancel the deal. I was all bombed out, and all day long, I kept thinking of all the time wasted inspecting the house and picking colors and money spent to find out the house was safe. I was angry and sad at myself, the bank, and the world for not doing things to work out for me.

And so, with this attitude of disgust, I had started the day and was trying to make it through the day. It was around 4 o'clock when my last patient walked into my dental office. A woman in her late thirties is usually very relaxed, easygoing, caring, and highly careful about the care of her kids. I had watched this woman go through her pregnancies with her two boys, and I had the opportunity to take care of the kids' dental treatments from the first year of their lives, which started 13 years ago.

Upon seeing me, I noticed tears started to gather up in the woman's eyes. What happened? I inquired quickly. I was expecting to hear something like I lost my job, or I lost money, or I lost my house, all equally significant events. But instead, she started to explain how she lost her 13-year-old son. He was riding his bicycle and got robbed, and the gang ended his life with a bullet discharged from a pistol and piercing his lung. I was sobbing over the loss of a house that I could not buy and live in now, but she was crying over the loss of her child, whom she had so diligently worked to raise for the past 13 years. I felt embarrassed to cry over what my loss was when I heard what her loss was and the long-term effect of it. All of a sudden, life was put into a different perspective. I felt shame for feeling towards the world the way I did, only because I had not managed to buy the house that I wanted. So much left to be grateful for.

CHAPTER 62
WHEN I WAS TOO AFRAID TO PUT UP A FIGHT
8/22/2009

This scenario kept on repeating itself in my life. Somebody would try to do me some wrong, and just because I didn't want things to get out of their peacefulness, I would close my eyes on what I wanted, what was right, and what mattered. Too many things were lost that way. To have peace, there was a greater price I was paying, the price of not doing the right thing. And so my life was going in the direction of haphazardness, no risks, no great challenges, no mountains to climb, and no battles to be fought. But also, that meant no wars to be won. And you see, winning and also losing are both part of an interesting life. Without any wins, life gets monotonous, and without any losses, there is no taste of the successes.

So, it all boiled down to this one summer day. Everything seemed to be stuck like in a jammed pair of teethed wheels. Nothing would move forward. It was one of those times in my life when it was one step forward and two steps backward. Every action I would take was matched with a reaction twice as large in the reverse. I was trying to do a bit of good. Something that would help everybody involved. I was fixing this broken area of driveway concrete in front of the rental house we had just moved into. From day one, when we moved into this house, there were challenges. Everything was broken and had to be fixed, and it was a big house, so things were twice as difficult to fix. I had asked this contractor to do the work that was benefiting everybody. My driveway was getting fixed, people and the mailman would not trip and fall anymore, the community would see a prettier driveway, the person I hired would put some food on the table for his family, and the person he hired to work for him got to have a life.

At the end of the day, when everything was almost finished, this random guy parked his car next to my driveway, got out, started to take pictures with his cell phone, and then showed me his badge from the city inspector. He asked me a bunch of questions, made me feel very intimidated, and told me to visit the city inspector's office the next day. I felt things were going terribly wrong all over again. I was getting ready to throw in the towel and concede the fight before it had even started. I lost all hope and demeanor.

But by nightfall, I realized the world was not over. At the end of the day, I had fixed my driveway, put food on the table of a family, and saved a few people from scrapes and wounds from tripping and falling. So now my only job was to fight with the city to make sure they understood that what I did had the good of everyone in mind and there was no basis for fining me or making my life any harder than it already was. I made myself push the fear away and accept the challenge, even if it meant losing the battle and paying a fine for not having applied for a permit. I knew I had done the right thing, so it didn't matter. I told myself I always just do the right thing, and the rest doesn't matter.

The next day, I found my way to City Hall to settle the case. The gentleman at the desk explained that my fine was over a thousand dollars, plus the fine for not cleaning after the concrete guy. I started to explain what had happened and what my purpose was, and even though I was at fault for not knowing I needed a permit for what minor repair had to be done, my project had saved people from falling, as was the case on many city streets where the tree roots had made the concrete sidewalk bulge out. I wasn't about to concede the fight to lessen my fine because I knew I had done the right thing.

The gentleman listened, and I was lucky to have had an honorable man listen to my reasoning. With each statement I made, he lessened the fine. Finally, we settled for $200, which I was happy to pay in the end because it represented my good faith in doing the right thing for the greater good of the people. Although the money mattered, being able to hold my head up when I walked out of the City Hall to stand up for the right cause and argue my case meant a lot more.

CHAPTER 63
DON'T LET THE SMALL STUFF GET IN THE WAY OF BIG STUFF
9/26/2009

Last night, a funny thing happened. My daughter picked up this desk and drawer set that we had ordered, and we discovered that it came totally unassembled, and we had to spend two hours to put it together. After spending the two hours, and of course, every bit of the way cursing at the person who sold this to me and didn't tell me that it was going to be so complicated to put it together, and also being mad at myself for not having told the guy to charge me extra and send someone to come and assemble it, I discovered that a piece was not working. The rollers would not fit into the hole they were supposed to. I tried to push and twist, and my son tried, and we all tried, but nothing worked. Now I was really mad because whatever time I thought I would have saved by doing this, the way I started would go to waste, and I would have to load it up in my car and take it to the shop and have them put it together.

Dinner started, albeit late because of our trek, and at dinner time, I was thinking of all the misery of the previous two hours. I was in a bad mood, and the dinner with my family, which should have been a time to treasure, went by like a wind. I was pushing myself deeper and deeper into anger and frustration. Dinner ended, and I went on the couch. While everybody went about doing their own stuff, I took a nap on the couch. I woke up and noticed my daughter was frantic about finishing the project, and rightly so because she had waited a whole month to get this thing, and now the thing was sitting unassembled and unfinished in a mess in the middle of her room. So, I got up and started to work on the project, trying to keep in mind that whatever I could put together would be one more step finished and closer to the end. Little by little, one more piece was finished, and with the help of my son, the project was nearly finished. It was 1 AM now, and everybody was really tired. I told myself I'll try one more time at the wheels. I took the hammer, and something guided me to hit it in the right place, and wham the thing popped in. In two minutes, the thing was done, and what had occupied my mind for a whole evening and an important dinner time was behind me. Was it worth the worry and the anger? Sometimes things have a way of resolving on their own, I whispered to myself. I was elated that I wouldn't have to drive to the shop the next day. The piece was almost finished now, and I just had to roll the drawers in when I noticed the whole thing was assembled upside down. Again, my mind started to race, especially since I had put glue in the wood connectors. But this time, I was equipped with the virtue of knowing that I could win. I snapped into action, knocked the sideboard out, unscrewed the hinges, and in ten minutes, what had taken me an hour to put together was unassembled and reassembled correctly.

It was really late at night now. Everybody was asleep. Job done, and life would be back to normal the next day, except that I had just lost having another memorable dinner with my family just because I couldn't close my eyes on the little stuff. Other than losing a bit of sleep time, nothing had been lost. Just wished I hadn't done all the huffing and puffing while I was working at it and preferably made a joke out of everything that went wrong and laughed about it with my kids.

Chapter 64
How do you make the right choice
9/26/2009

When presented with two choices, how do you know which one is the right one or the better one? Should one look as to what is the best choice for today and right now, or what is the best choice for tomorrow or years later? I realize that through time, we change, and because of that, our choices and preferences may change.

I have two offices that I practice out of in two areas of town. For the past twenty years, this has given me a sense of security, knowing that I have two groups of patients that I can depend on. Knowing that if another earthquake hits and one office building gets destroyed, as happened in the 1994 earthquake in Los Angeles to one of my colleagues, I can depend on the other one to quickly allow me to do my work. Of course, it is a hassle to have the two offices. I can't be on top of everything as well as I would want to be. I have two leases and two buildings to deal with and two sets of everything else. So, now that my lease is up, I am wondering what to do. My office furniture is old and needs to be replaced. Is it worth the hassle? But I really need the little bit of extra income that this office brings in order to be able to afford and qualify for a loan to buy my house. So it is with a heavy heart that I decided to keep the second office and still work out of there and continue to deal with the hassles of occupying an old office in an old building.

Fast forward five years, my lease is up again, and I have to go through all the same emotions and thoughts that I had to go through last time. Except now I have my home, and I don't have to depend on that extra income so much to qualify for the loan immediately. I do need to eventually have the income to support my payments, but a few months of downtime is manageable, and eventually, I can build the office I keep, supporting me the way I need it to.

So, times have changed. Priorities have changed. Needs have changed. The choice I made was the best for the time, and now I have a better choice for today to bring me a better result. I should feel safe to change course and make a move to better my life. I just have to be careful not to hurt any feelings in the process.

CHAPTER 65
BAD LUCK OR GOOD LUCK
10/13/2009

I often wondered to myself what defined bad luck and what good luck has been had. Here is what I mean.

October 13th, and I was in this town I was unfamiliar with. Upon nightfall I decided to go out to dinner. I found this nice restaurant, had a dinner that was very average, then got into my rental car, a small, flimsy Hyundai, and decided to drive around town a little bit. After about 20 minutes, I decided it was enough driving and started to drive back to my hotel. Driving down the road, the GPS said you had now reached your destination. I looked up, and it seemed I was missing the entrance to my hotel. It required a rapid, sharp turn to get into the narrow street on the left. I looked ahead, but there were no oncoming cars; therefore, I thought it safe to make the rapid turn. It was late at night, on a quiet street where not too many cars go by. A quick, instantaneous decision, and I initiated the turn. To my bad luck, there happened to be a middle lane on this unknown street that was designated for buses. Right at that instant, that split second, there happened to be a bus at my side, and as I made the turn, a bus ran into the side of my car. It hit my car right at the junction of the driver's door and front fender to do the most damage. It hit me so hard that it gave my car a sudden jolt, airbags opening 360 degrees around me and creating a big mess. When the airbags opened, it felt like someone punched me in the face. I came out of the car and couldn't believe the damage to my car and the bus. I wasn't going that fast; how could all this have happened? My car is so tiny, and the bus so big; how could my car cause so much damage to the bus? The bus had to be towed away. I felt so unlucky. Imagine the street at 10 o'clock at night, all empty, and

I am driving along. At the same instant that I decide to make a turn, a bus happens to be next to me. Busses probably don't pass that spot any sooner than once every 10 minutes at that time of the night, and there are 600 seconds in that 10 minutes and one second sooner for my turn; I would have turned before the bus had a chance to get close to me, and one second later, the bus would have seen me turn and stopped in time to avoid hitting me, but my bad luck it had to happen at the same exact second that would cause this terrible accident. I felt really unlucky.

But there is another side to the story.

On October 13th, at nightfall, I decided to go out to dinner. I found this nice restaurant, had a dinner that was very average, then got into my car and decided to drive around town a little bit. After about 20 minutes, I decided it was enough driving and started to drive back to my hotel. Driving down the road, the GPS said you had now reached your destination. I looked, and it seemed I was missing the entrance to my hotel. It required a rapid, sharp turn to get into the narrow street. I looked ahead, but there were no oncoming cars; therefore, I thought it safe to make the rapid turn. It was late at night, on a quiet street where not too many cars go by. A quick, instantaneous decision, and I initiated the turn. Unfortunately, there happened to be a middle lane with a bus in it, and at that same instant, as I was turning, the bus was right at my side. The bus ran into the side of my small, tiny car. Luckily, the side airbags opened up and saved my face from injury. I got out of my car, and I couldn't believe the damage to the car and the bus. The bus had hit me at the edge of the front door and fender. I thought to myself, this is an empty street at this time of the night, and if this bus had hit me a tenth of a second later, it would have hit me right into my door, probably injuring me and causing my car to flip over due to the high speed of the bus. So many seconds in 10 minutes and 6000 tenths of seconds in

10 minutes, and I was saved only by a magic tenth of a second that could have changed everything. I felt really lucky.

Yes, there is a very fine line between lucky and unlucky. But that fine line becomes even cloudier when you look at the same event from a different angle. So, how do you feel today?

CHAPTER 66
GOOD LUCK OPTIMISM
12/12/2009

I was lying on the bed on the second floor of my house on this rainy, gloomy day. I was reading this book about luck. It mentioned the contrast between lucky and unlucky people in the world in the way they actually view events that happen to them. Lucky people see bad events as how much worse they could have been and then feel happy that it wasn't the worst thing that happened, and therefore, they get happy, but unlucky people see the event and say why me? And so they feel bad.

I started to look back into my life to see if there was any time in my life that I considered myself lucky. Was there any time that I was amongst the lucky group of people, and then when was it or what happened that changed me from one category to the other? An instantaneous memory that comes to my mind is when my mother had a car accident and was in the intensive care unit after a 3-hour operation because of her badly broken leg and foot. I was watching her breathe, hoping that she would open her eyes soon so I could give her the good news that the doctors could save her leg. In the wee hours of the morning, after a long night of waiting, she moved her head and opened her eyes slightly. "I can't move my legs she said" with a worrisome look on her face. "I know", I said, "you have two huge casts on your legs, the doctors could save both of your legs, but you will have the casts on for a while. You still have your own legs, isn't that great." She looked at her toes that were sticking out from the cast and once reassured that she could still wiggle them, she closed her eyes and went back to sleep. I look at myself and the events of that day; there was nothing lucky about that day or its events. A freak accident led to this dim hospital room and a lot of unknowns for our future. What in the world could be lucky about it? Yet, still, at that time in my life, I was able to look at life with optimism and a sense that we were lucky because it could have been worse. So, when did my optimism change to pessimism and fear and feelings of unluckiness?

A week later, as my mom was healing in the hospital, she expressed her fear about the possible result of her accident. I assured her that since this was not a disease process and it was only a trauma and accident, and the surgery had been completed successfully, she was going to recover fine and there was nothing to worry about, and it was only a matter of time before she would be up and running. I was still an optimist.

A month or two went by, and she was getting better. By that time, I had noticed this lump growing in my neck. A few days and an MRI later, I found out that I had a tumor in my neck. We sought a surgeon, and he said we had to take it out ASAP. I was still an optimist. I was telling everyone else that there was nothing to worry about, and this was probably a plain, simple growth that had to be taken out. Just another surgical procedure, I thought to myself. I'll heal from it quickly. I have a good, strong body, and I have never smoked or drunk, so it can't be a bad tumor. I had still kept it a secret from my mom, thinking that after the surgery, I could just tell her it was an accident and I needed a few stitches in my neck. A few days before the surgery, however, the result of the biopsy suggested that the tumor was cancerous. What do I do now? I thought to myself. A month earlier, I was telling my mom not to worry because her condition is not a disease, and, therefore, there is nothing to worry about, and she is going to heal fast. How do I explain this disease and my chances of healing to her now? This is a disease. How in the world am I now going to convince her that I am going to heal from this, so she won't worry? I still had every confidence that I was going to go through this treacherous surgery and heal from it uneventfully. I was still an optimist. I believed all was going to be well. Still considered myself lucky, even though my doctors could not tell exactly what type of cancerous tumor was growing in my neck.

The surgery day came and went, and as I had suspected, I was on the road to recovery very fast. I had amazed myself and everyone around me as to how easy this surgery had been, although it had been quite complicated. I was on cloud nine when my surgeon reported that the tumor seemed to be a single solid mass and there was no evidence of it on the PET scans anywhere else in my body, and that he had successfully removed the whole tumor in one piece. Lucky again, I thought to myself.

A few weeks later, the final result of the biopsy came in. My tumor was a very rare and highly malignant cancerous tumor, it said. No one really knows how to treat this, except perhaps some radiation to the neck, just in case. Then, this specialist, who happened to be in Los Angeles at the time, came along. This kind of tumor was his cup of tea, a few doctors told me. A consultation with him revealed that I needed to have nine months of chemotherapy. When I inquired as to how it would be, my specialist told me not to worry; I would get the chemo every few weeks, and I could go to work in between. "Then okay," I said speedily; when do we start? I want to get this thing behind me as soon as possible. I was still an optimist. I still see the bright side that this highly cancerous tumor had not spread anywhere else in my body despite its tennis ball size in my neck.

But then the chemo started, and I started to get really sick from it, and I couldn't go to work or even lead a semi-normal life for the duration of the treatment. My body became very weak after the treatment, and my life had been turned inside out at the age of 38 with two little children at home and a mom who was trying to recover from a horrific accident. My trust, faith, and optimism were fading away. I was starting to ask why me. I was starting to imagine what should have been instead of seeing what it was. I now wonder if that is when I started to feel unlucky instead of lucky. Perhaps that is when this belief of unluckiness started to follow me around. A simple series of unlucky events. How do I shake it off of me now, I wonder?

But I must. There is much to behold and look forward to. Optimism has to take over.

CHAPTER 67
INTERESTING PHENOMENON
1/20/2010

Mathematical equations and statistical probabilities attest to the fact that if you have a jar with different items of nearly similar size when mixed together in equal numbers, you have the same chance of picking any one of the items each time you reach into the jar. Furthermore, if you keep picking the same item time after time, then you reduce the chances of picking that same item in your future picks, and you increase the chance of picking the other items.

Put to the test, this theory might not prove so correct. Or it may prove that other factors do come into play. While I drive back from work, to keep me occupied while I wait in traffic, I have a bag with a mixture of almonds, walnuts, cashew nuts, and dried cranberries. When I filled up this bag at the market, I put equal numbers of these in the bag. I noticed, though, that each time I reach into the bag to pick a few items, although I dig around, I usually come out with more walnuts than any other item and almost never with any cranberries. This happened a few days in a row, so it caught my attention. Even though after a few days, there were even fewer walnuts in the bag than on day one, I still came out with more walnuts. If I wanted cranberries, I had to specifically search for them and pick them out from the crowd. Why was this so, I thought to myself. Shouldn't I have the same number of each item in my hand when I pull it out of the bag? The laws of probabilities had changed, influenced by other factors. So the cranberries, since they were smaller, were sinking to the bottom of the bag, lessening my chance of coming up with them, and the walnuts, since they were the biggest and most irregular in shape and size and texture, were having the greatest chance of getting picked.

Time after time and day after day, the sweet cranberries were being missed, and the dry, rough walnuts were being picked.

So now I wonder to myself, is this the way it is with real life, too? Although it has an equal mixture of good and bad, sweet and sour, bitter and flavorful moments, the bad and the ugly get picked more often, and they stand out in the crowd and in our view of life more often. No matter how we twist our fingers in the bag of life, we are bound to pick out the events and experiences with rough edges more often. But there is a silver lining to all of this. When all the walnuts and almonds were gone, I kept picking sweet cranberries one after another. In the end, many sweet moments and experiences were being had.

CHAPTER 68
ANOTHER MAN'S JOURNEY INTO LIFE
1/29/2010

Into my office walked this man. He has been my patient for at least 20 years. A nice, polite, handsome guy. I have seen him go through many stages of life. I was marveling about my journey into life and where my life stood at age 51 when this guy walked into my office with a tooth problem. You see, I used to think of tooth problems as such a big thing until I saw what things can really happen in one's life. Then the tooth problem really became a small thing, but it is still a big thing in this guy's life, with everything else that he has gone through.

A successful businessman in his hometown was thrown in jail for some stupid reason when the revolution happened in his country. Most of his assets were confiscated. Then he came to the United States, only to lose his million dollars of savings in a real estate deal that turned sour. The land that he purchased went underwater and became worthless, and he was forced to sell it along with his partners for almost nothing. Ironically, a few years later, the land became worth ten times its original value; he would have become a multimillionaire had he kept the land, but too late.

Then, he was diagnosed with cancer, the kind that will not go away. He has had it for ten years now, going through a few series of heavy chemotherapies over the years, but is still surviving, probably only to give me a lesson in survival. He has managed to raise two great kids who are as well-mannered as he is. He doesn't smile often, but when he gets ready to leave my office, he looks like he is wearing the mentality of a fighter to step out there in the real world. He continues to care a lot about his teeth. To him, with everything he has gone through, they are still just as important as they were on day one when he came to me. He never looks at what the end might look like, and he doesn't let the status of the day remove his integrity. Maybe God sent him to me for a reason: to know and see how resilient a man can be, to never give up despite all the trash cards that life deals us. He keeps shaking off the dirt on his back and rises to the top.

CHAPTER 69
WHAT HAPPENED TO UNITED
4/10/2010

It has been a nerve-racking year in America. All sorts of people have lost money, belongings, peace of mind, serenity, direction, and will. But most of all, there is one element that has totally disappeared from society. I think to myself, what did ever happen to the sense of mutual cooperation? What happened to the United in the United States of America? There was a time when students would stand behind each other to protect one another; now, they bully and cause death. Landlords and tenants no longer wish to think of win-win situations, only what makes them the most money in the shortest time. No one cares about who loses a business they have worked on for so many years, neither the jobs that have supported families for almost a lifetime or helped a business grow to its highest peak. Parents and kids go their own separate ways without mutual support and love. Republicans are against Democrats without regard for what is at stake. Everybody is trying to fulfill their dreams without care and caution for the others involved. Whatever happened to that feeling and desire for mutual cooperation? Who is benefiting from all of this? No one. Everyone ends up losing at the end. Workers lose their jobs, owners lose their businesses, landlords lose their properties, banks lose their loans, the government ends up paying more and receiving less and doing less, a stalemate in the parliament, and the country is paralyzed.

Nothing will improve until everybody realizes that no one benefits from this ordeal, and the only way to get over it is to try to find common ground and work up from there. I think the only way we can the history this bump in the history of the country is to realize that without mutual cooperation and compromises, we all stand to lose a lot, not just financially but also the moral fabric of our society which has so strongly been built over the years.

151

CHAPTER 70
LIFE CHANGING............
5/6/2010

Last weekend, I went to our usual friend's bicycle at the beach and beach volleyball event. Everything seemed to be like another usual Sunday morning. Arrive at 8:30 with my friend, meet the others, and start bicycling for an hour, then start the volleyball game. During the game, as usual, I started to daydream. My play level had not been good lately, actually, for the past 20 years, and I would lose faith and confidence very fast, and as soon as I lost a couple of points, I would concede the match and all effort to win. I was daydreaming about that doomed volleyball game in my 11th grade. We were destined to get 1st place in my high school. Just a couple of points left, and with the other team missing some of their star players due to injury, we were presumed to be the absolute winners. My turn to serve, and again, I did one of my sloppy serves into the net. I had good serves, but every time I went to the serving line, my whole body was filled with doubt. And this time, not only was it not an exception, but the element of overconfidence also added to it. The points were lost, and the rest of the points were lost by one member of my team or another, and to everybody's astonishment, we lost the game. Just like that, the gold medal slipped from our hands. As I was deeply reviewing this video in full color in my head, my friend screamed at me. "Hey, where are you, it's your turn to serve," he said. I picked up the ball and moved behind the line. I was telling myself, "Oh no, not again, I'm going to serve it right into the net again." After all, why should this serve to be any different from the one before it and the ones from last weekend? Even though I know how to serve killer serves, I miss 4 out of 5 of them.

As I was rolling the ball in my hand, a thought came to my mind. What if I could hit a real killer serve, one of those life-changing serves? So I told myself: "Hey look, this is your chance to hit one of those life-changing serves. You are not going to miss it. Just do it the best you can. Have no fear and do it." I tossed the ball up in the air and mumbled to myself, here is a life-changing serve. It turned out to be an awesome hit, and they couldn't return it. I served again, mumbling, "Here is a life-changing serve," again to myself as I hit another shot that left everyone gasping for air. One after another, five winners in a row, life-changing serves. I was amazed at this life-changing experience. Does it really work, I wondered? After a few rotations, it was my turn again, and of course, the famous words were repeated just before the serve. "You are on a roll today," everyone shouted. Aside from being very happy that I could serve consistently killer serves again, I was elated that I had finally discovered that the reason my life was in a rut was that I was not willing to put my willpower into a life-changing action. If I want an amazing result, I must be willing to perform at a life-changing level.

I went home and on a big piece of paper wrote "LIFE CHANGING..............," and hung it on the wall on top of my desk. So now, every day, when I want to take an action in a way that shows how much I desire the best and highest outcome from it, I will say: Here is a life-changing action. Then I know that I have committed 100% to that action I want to take, and now I can expect results instead of having doubts. I can finally be a winner again.

Chapter 71
The best or the last
6/6/2010

I was traveling through time at my usual pace- which truthfully seems a lot faster these days than before- and I was tired of being in my usual rut. I have been thinking to myself, I need something new, different; I need to get alive. I have just been traveling the road, day by day, overwhelmed by life itself.

Then, suddenly, a thought came to my mind. What if I decide as to whether this is going to be the best or the last year of my life? What would I choose? Which one would I want it to be? Now, let's make a choice: blue pill or red pill; if I could pick one, which would it be? Suppose I had a choice to make this the best or the last year of my life; which one would I choose? The answer was obvious to me: I wanted it to be the best. I already am a seasoned person, and I know that life can have terrible ups and downs and plenty of hurdles along the way, but what if I lived it as if it were the last year of my life, and therefore, it had to be turned into the best year of my life. Do I want to sit still and choose one of my previous years of life to be my best, or do I want to make this a new best year of my life? I vote for a new beginning, a new day, a new year. Let us make it different and do stuff; maybe it will be the best, maybe it won't, but it is worth a try.

All I have to do is to be courageous and take a 10% improvement step each day. Just one act each day that would make that day 10% better than it would have been. Make plans that would turn your week fabulous and your month superb, and when you look to the past quarter or season, you'll say, "Man, what a blast".

CHAPTER 72
NEED HELP
6/19/2010

The other day, I was thinking to myself, "Whatever happened to that sense of mutual cooperation and consideration?".

When was it that myself and I became more important than us? Everybody has turned out to be out there for themselves and for their own benefit. True, there are still a few Good Samaritan volunteers left out there who go and truthfully help other people, but more and more, I come across people who pretend they are there for the benefit of others but are actually trying to benefit the "me."

As I walk around the city, I see the parking enforcement guy writing tickets as fast as he can to benefit himself again, not hesitating for a moment that the $50 taken away from that poor car owner could have been the result of a day's worth of work, or the grocery money he needed to feed his children. Two minutes late, and he is out of luck. Then, the city was looking out for itself when they raised the meter fees to $1 per 15 minutes, not thinking about what would happen to the store owners when people got fed up with feeding the meter and stayed away from the business areas. I guess we don't care, just as long as my needs are met. I see the doctor who has worked so hard to become a doctor and now is forced to perform procedures because, again, he is thinking of himself and doesn't take into consideration what he is charging the poor patient and is so out of whack with what the person makes and needs. True, insurance pays for it, but then again, we come back to the same "me, myself, and I" who put his corporate profits before the organization and maintaining fair practices so both the doctor and patient could benefit from less time wasted, money thrown away, and patient care lost. Maybe, after all, we do need that health care reform, but then I worry whether this will be another one of those things where it looks good in the beginning, and then little by little, pieces of the pie are taken away to benefit the many I's. And, oh yes, this is a good one. What about all those internet sites that appear to be helping you and operating for your benefit, but their underlying agenda is to veer you to their affiliated business to make their own "Mine" money? I know what you are thinking: that is the way business works: advertise, get your face out there and be recognized, and then make the money; that's capitalism. But that is not what I am talking about. If you are a true capitalist, don't hide your identity and agenda behind a screen; show the truth and let the best provider and business win. I also understand that many create a win-win situation, but if that is your intention, again, don't hide; make your affiliations clear.

It was heartbreaking when I saw the oil leak on the bottom of the ocean. All that effort that so many millions of people put into keeping a clean environment free of pollutants and dangerous chemicals is wiped out by one simple act of negligence. For years to come, millions of people and a multitude of locations will suffer, just like it happened in Chornobyl. I really need help. I can't understand how these people put "me, myself, and I" before everybody else. And, oh yes, do you remember the mortgage meltdown? A bunch of people went on a borrowing and spending spree, not thinking who was going to pay for all this debt. "I don't care who gets stuck with the bill. As long as I get what I want now". Then, as we saw, we all suffered, both the perpetrators and the bystanders, again for years to come. When are we as a society going to learn that whatever we do has consequences, and it will come back to haunt us if we don't think of the greater good before committing ourselves to action? Of course, if we are committed to winning a soccer match, we don't have to think of the greater good; just a win-it mentality is acceptable. Or is it? Disappointing our fans and viewers by playing a bad game doesn't get fixed by the fact that the game was won. The sense of disappointment will last a long time in our memories when performance is smeared by dishonesty.

Chapter 73
The perfect number 7
10/10/2010

A few days ago, my aunt passed away. She was married to my uncle and had been in a coma for almost a year and a half. My uncle passed away a few years ago, and they had an amazingly close and sweet relationship during their life together. At her funeral, I learned that she passed away the same day as my uncle, just a couple of years apart. I was thinking to myself, what an amazing concept; how do two people so close choose to leave their earthly life in coincidence with each other? I also lost the father of one of my colleagues that week. It was a somber week as it was raining throughout. I had been thinking of my own mom's passing again, questioning why she left when she did. It looked like such an imperfect time according to my plans and calendar. I mean, which grandmother leaves in between the birthdays of two grandchildren who celebrate birthdays two weeks apart and so close to her own daughter's birthday; everything looked imperfect.

The next day, as I was entering the Temple for my friend's father's memorial service, the head Rabbi of the synagogue was giving a speech. As he was relating the passing of the person who had lived a very honorable life compared to a perfect life, he started to say how the number 7 is so perfect. Suddenly, I had a click in my head. You see, I always wondered why my mother died in July, the seventh month of the year because July is a time of celebration, not sorrow. The Hebrew date was the 27th of the month of Sivan. Coincidence, you think? 27th and Sivan sound much like seven. Oh yes, and then why July of the year 1997? Did I forget to say that the Jewish year was the year 5757? I started to put it all together on 7/2/1997, which is the

27th of Sivan in the year 5757. Incidentally, I have read in my mother's writings that the recorded birthday for her is not really 1919; she was really born in the year 1920 but was given the birth records of a sister who passed after birth a year earlier. She always insisted that her birthday was in the year 1920 and not 1919 as was recorded. If she is correct, then that puts her age at 77. I can't help but start to think that for her, that was a perfect time.

In all my sadness, I started to realize how, for the past thirteen years since her passing, her anniversary has coincided with important events. According to the Jewish calendar, the day moves around every year by a month or so sometimes. I remembered the time that it coincided with my wedding anniversary, my kid's birthdays, my niece's wedding anniversary, my other niece's wedding events, Father's Day, graduations, and so on. Each year, as we come to see what the date of her passing anniversary is, I notice it coincides with something going on. I now start to think that maybe there was something perfectly magic about that day when she decided to leave. Her soul gets to be present at many significant events in the lives of her children and grandchildren. She gets to celebrate many worldly events with us. After all, maybe there was something perfect about 7.

CHAPTER 74
ADVISING MY KIDS
10/17/10

My kids have grown up now and are both in college. They are still my children, and as such, I still see the need to offer guidance many times. It is hard, but I am trying to find a balance between being a supporter and being a nag. Every time I see something that needs fixing, I think twice before I offer my help. But I am not sure if that is the best way because a lot of times, I miss the opportunity to offer guidance in time, and they make mistakes that could have easily been prevented. I know that life is all about making mistakes and growing from your mistakes, but I think that is a cliché that doesn't hold. Instead of making mistakes and growing from your mistakes, how about choosing the right choice and building on top of success? So I think to myself, which would be more motivating and uplifting, to fail and learn and move on, or to succeed and learn and take the next step, which would result in greater accomplishment and speedier achievements. One would think that once you fail, the learning process would become so deeply ingrained to prevent future failures, but if you never fail, you do not learn, and you will proceed without caution, and sooner or later, you will meet a failing point and that will be more painful. But I suggest that the fewer failures one experiences in a process or in life, the greater the chances of higher achievement. Failure may be good, but too many of them will act as a brake to making quick decisions and self-confidence. A greater ratio of proper successful choices to wrong ones, and the person will be more encouraged to take chances and develop a more positive attitude to taking steps and accomplishing goals.

It is also true that the younger we are, the greater the chances that we process failures differently and forget the negative faster and move on, whereas when we are older, we become more cautious and hence more cognizant of our failing or wrong decisions. As such, I have tried to put situations in front of my kids that would stimulate the good result of positive experiences. Sometimes, though, I let things go, especially on not-too-important things; my daughter wanted to buy a bicycle to use at school. I could have taught her everything about how to protect it from getting stolen. But as an experiment, I decided to let her travel through the process. She bought the bicycle, and when it was stolen within the first week, I felt that I should have taught her so that she would not make a mistake. She bought a second one, and again, I let her grow up on her own. Again, it was stolen within a week. All this because I, as an experienced bicycle owner, did not take the time to help her not make the mistake again. I did not want to intervene in her life. More importantly, I did not want her to feel that I was intervening in her life.

But the result was the unnecessary experience of loss, which caused her pain rather than growth. There is a fine line between interference and support to grow, and one should find a proper balance between the two.

CHAPTER 75
THE BOY WHO COULD
10/19/10

I was having dinner with my wife at a Chinese restaurant. As we finished, we were served the regular fortune cookies that appeared on the bill. My wife speedily cracked her cookie, tossed the paper, and started to eat the cookie. I, on the other hand, broke the cookie, took the paper in between my fingers, held it real tight, and told my wife: "We believe whatever this says, agree?" My wife nodded in support of my suggestion, so I slowly removed my fingers and started to read the fortune cookie. It said: "If you think you can do something, you are right; if you think you can't do something, you are right."

My wife, being as positive a person as she is, immediately thought out loud. See, if you believe something, it will happen the way you believe it will. Your choice is to believe it will happen and it will happen or believe it won't happen and it won't. However, for me it was a different story. I started to think more philosophically. My thinking was that the Chinese masters believe so much in building self-confidence that what they are trying to say in this fortune cookie is that you are right no matter what. Trust your intuition. Believe in yourself. Have self-confidence. If you think you can do something, you are right; you can do it. And if your gut feeling is that you can't do something, your gut feeling is right; don't think otherwise.

I could see bewilderment and unacceptance in my wife's face. Instantly, an event that had taken place the previous weekend came to my mind. I had been coaching 12-year-old kids' soccer. There is this one kid on my team who came with very little soccer knowledge and ability. For the first three weeks of the season, I tried to get him to come out of his shell and do something. Still, the team would go out on the field, and he would be the same timid player, quite unable to make any moves on the ball or other players. Then, one lucky day, I ended up giving a ride to a few of the kids on my team. During the ride, as I was trying to pry out info from the kids to know more about them, this kid told me that he was afraid that he would do something wrong on the field. That was the break I was looking for. Just before the next game started, I went up to the kid and said: "Mr. P., I want you to go out there and know that there is nothing that you can do that is wrong, even if you foul somebody, it is not wrong. Whatever you do is the right thing. Believe and truly believe that whatever you do is okay and is the right thing to do, and you are right about doing it."

The game started, and I was amazed at how this kid was performing. All of a sudden, he was a different person. He was running to the ball, engaging other players, and being a very useful person on the team. This went on for the first half of the game. At halftime, I congratulated him and told him how pleased I was that he was participating more. The second half started, and this kid who would normally be all tired up after a quarter period of running was still going at it full steam. Then suddenly, disaster struck. My assistant coach, unaware of what I had discovered some days earlier and what my strategy was with this kid, noticed that he was being active in the wrong area of the field. He shouted his name out and told him to go to his spot and stick with it. All of a sudden, I saw the kid roll back into his shell. He folded his arms into his chest, crouched over, and stood motionless in the spot that he was assigned. Except for that, he was now a useless member of the team again. In an instant, he had been stripped of his freedom to do what he thought might be right and what he was free to do. I realized that at some point, he had probably been criticized for what he had done, and that was what was stopping him from finding his true potential. I went closer to him and asked him to come to the side of the field so I could talk to him. I told him to ignore the assistant coach and to only listen to me. I confirmed with him again that there is nothing that he can do that is wrong. Just like magic, I saw the kid start to be active and show his talent again.

That is when I discovered that it truly matters to build self-confidence in kids by making them believe that they are capable of doing the right thing, no matter what. Stop criticizing and judging them and let them be, even if it means making some mistakes along the way.

CHAPTER 76
IN SPIRIT
11/13/10

Last night, we were at my brother's for the traditional Friday night dinner. A few guests there, 6 or 7 families altogether. Everybody was having drinks and gathering in groups to converse about the day's events and recent news. I stepped out of the room and went into the beautiful yard. The air was crisp and clean. The temperature was just perfect, so one could comfortably sit and enjoy the beautiful, colorful design of the plants and flowers. The fire pit was on and gave off just enough warmth to add to the perfect setting. The flames kept dancing up and down so as to make the setting look alive and real. In fact, though, I was experiencing a surreal life.

As I sat out there in the quiet peacefulness, nobody was aware of my absence in the room. Life still kept going on. The faint noise of conversations still seeped out through the half-open yard door. It seemed as if even when you were gone, no one would notice you were not there. Life will go on, and no one will sense you or touch you. They will only miss you when they get reminded of your memory, but otherwise, they can live a complete life. Moreover, when I want to see and feel them, all I have to do is for my spirit to be present, even if it is in a slightly remote location from where everyone is gathered. I can look through the window and see my wife and daughter laughing; I can see my brother sharing thoughts and emotions with my cousins and other family members, each doing their own thing. I can experience and feel everything that is going on in that house without anybody even being aware of my presence or absence, for that matter. When I am there in spirit, I can see and hear everything and enjoy watching everybody without them even knowing I am there, without even disturbing or redirecting their lives. This is amazing. It may feel that I am gone, but in reality, I can still be there for as long as I want.

So is this what my parents, who are now gone, maybe doing? Is it possible that even at this very moment, one of them is sitting right next to me and is seeing and feeling everything that is going on in this house the same exact way that I am?

Chapter 77
Then and Now
10/27/2010

It is the day after Thanksgiving, and I am lying on the couch in the den and staring out the window into the yard. There is a line of trees at the far end of the yard. Tall, thick, green cypress trees that were probably planted 50 years ago and have grown to become a hefty piece of this property.

I remember it was two years ago when we were in our previous house. Lying down on the couch, I would look out the window into the yard, and I would see the trees at the end of the yard that had been trimmed by the landlord so terribly that all you could see were bare branches. It was so depressing and low energy. Winter was starting, and the combination of the small yard and the ugly trees made a bad match.

Today, I have turned halfway around. The luscious green trees add energy and liveliness to the day. It certainly feels good to have what there is. It is coming to me at a great cost, but if I were here only for this short period of time, then this makes it all worth it. This makes me think it is the continuity of life that makes it so hard to live the way that we feel is best for us. If we were only living today, we could live it differently. If we have to think of tomorrow, there are certain precautions we have to and want to take. This makes me think as to how much more difficult living in today's world has become. We know that we have to live this life probably for something between 80 and 100 years and that by itself has added a great burden of planning and holding back on how to live. When I was a child, I remember people used to live 50 or 60 years, rarely over 80. So they knew that in the short life they had, they could use their fruit of productivity right away and live as if there was no tomorrow. That made them live more day-to-day and possibly happier lives.

It is not how many years of life we have ahead of us to live; it is the way we live those years. Do we stare at the small, beautiful things that surround us and don't cost any money, or do we keep chasing the perpetual wheel to find something big at the top of the pole that doesn't matter to anyone if nobody is there to see it or if there is nobody around to share it with? Imagine being the King of a country that has no population. You are the King, but there is not a single person in the kingdom. Does it matter anymore that you are the King? It only matters that you are a King if there are followers and if your being a King will, in one way or another, have an effect on someone else. What if you are not the King of the kingdom and you are just a simple commoner? Does it then matter if there is a King to rule over you versus if everyone is a commoner? If all the commoners are as knowledgeable and ethical as you and a King- in other words, everyone is worthy of being a King- will you then be better off having a King or living in a place where all the people are kings?

So, what defines a King? He who can do more than others, or he who knows more than others, or he who can rule over others, or he who has more followers, or he who finds a balance between making something of their life at the same time that they stare at the trees from their couch. Right now, it feels like I am the King.

CHAPTER 78
THE STRANGE HAPPENINGS
12/11/10

I woke up, and somehow, I could feel it wasn't going to be what I wanted it to be. I thought to myself whether I should go back to sleep and wake up again. Maybe things will be in synchronicity when I wake up again. I didn't go back to sleep and pushed myself to get up and continue.

Went to the kitchen to make some eggs. I put the egg out of the carton onto the countertop. As I turned around to put the box in the refrigerator, the egg rolled off and fell to the floor and shattered.

I finished my breakfast in the den. Tried to clean up the table from some cups and plates that had been there from the night before. I picked up this green glass and then went for the peanut butter jar. I could feel it was wrong. Continued still. The green glass fell onto the glass table and shattered.

My kid's soccer game started at 1 PM. The referee was examining the kids with such detail. Again, I knew there was something not right. The game started. A game that we should have won. There was no score in the first half, no score in the second half, and no score overtime, heading to penalty kicks. I had five great kickers; 3 of them missed. We still tied and went to the sixth shooter. He shot too high and missed. The other team scored and won.

The next day, I was refereeing a championship game. Suddenly, I saw flames break out through the balcony of the top floor of the Hi-Rise apartment building across the street. It was amazing.

Unusual happenings all piled up in one weekend. I should have gone back to sleep and started over. Maybe things would have been different altogether if I had listened to my initial gut feeling.

Chapter 79
High Expectations vs. Power of Intention
12/31/10

I was evaluating the year and my accomplishments. I had goals set and desires written down. Where do I stand now that a year has gone by? Expectations have been had, some fulfilled and some not. Desires were written down, some forgotten, and some no longer desired. Intentions imagined, part fantasy, and part realistic.

So now I am thinking to myself, is it better to have high expectations or no expectations? If you have high expectations and then you don't get them, then the few that you didn't get stand out in comparison to the achieved ones and then make you disappointed. The glass-half-empty syndrome. But if you don't have any expectations yet, you set goals and constantly work to achieve them, then whatever you achieve gets a checkmark, and then it stands out as all the things you did, and you feel good. The question comes when you tell yourself that you need to have intentions in this universe so that what you want eventually materializes. I have noticed that some intentions easily materialize. I am thinking of meeting someone, and then it happens. Looking for a parking spot in the most unusual circumstances, and it's there. But then some intentions, no matter how valid and how reasonable to have and think of, do not come true. What is in the thought that creates the difference? Is having a lot of intentions equal to having a lot of expectations? Are expectations created in a different way and thus have a different energy attached to them? Are intentions received by the universe on a different wavelength, and thus, when they fall into harmony with the process and vibration of the universe, become reality easily?

Okay, honestly, I have had this expectation of winning the lottery for some time. I really want to say that I have intended to be the winner of the lottery. If I expect, it means I am not in harmony with the universe. But if I intend, it means I very much like it if it were to happen, allowing the universe to flow in ways it needs to flow to make it happen. I need to know that nature is much stronger and much smarter than me, and if I allow it to perform in ways that are harmonious with its flow, then it can find its own way of making this happen for me.

It is like a want, a wish, a desire, and above all, a justified, heartfelt knowing that it will happen for me.

CHAPTER 80
WHAT IS THE POINT OF LIFE
1/2/2011

It was a dark day outside. It had been raining most of the day, with black clouds covering the horizon. My daughter had been studying most of the morning, and she was getting frustrated with making heads and tails out of the nonsense in her textbooks. All of a sudden, she asked: "Dad, what is the point of life?"

I turned inward and thought to myself for a minute. I wanted to be philosophical and say it is to get good grades, become somebody in your life, and be proud of your achievements. No, that would be too fatherly. Then I thought maybe I should answer on a higher level, think about the good of society, and say that the point of life is to create a better world for the people around us. But that is not what I feel today; maybe it was the way I used to think when I was younger, and I actually thought that people around me cared for each other. Then I thought maybe it would be better if I just gave her choices. I thought I would rant about how, for some people, the point of life is to make money, while for others, it is to build a building, paint a painting, or raise a family. This made me think to myself, though, which one of these is my point of life. I have had one or another of them in my thoughts at different times in my life. It all changes from time to time. But the point of life can't change from time to time. It has to always be the same. So, what is the point of life?

I thought I would get smart and turn the table on her, so I asked her: "What is the point of your life." Without delay, she said: "I am all lost; there doesn't seem to be a point to live. It just comes and goes, like a bubble." By now, I knew I had to make something good come out of this conversation. I had to make this rainy day count. I have to be honest and fearless. I have to let life arrange itself as it wishes in a manner that will have meaning to her a week from now, a year from now, or even ten years from now. My eyes suddenly caught the fireplace gently burning in the corner of the living room. I turned to my daughter and told her what I thought would be an answer that would hold true at any time or stage of life.

I told her that life is like a fireplace, and it needs new logs to keep burning, and the point of life is to keep it burning. In order to keep it burning, you have to feed it, and what it needs to keep burning is good experiences. This is the true point of life. To feed it with good, profound experiences. Live your life fully, enjoy the moments, and create good moments of good experiences for yourself because it is by you experiencing good moments that you keep feeding logs to the fireplace of your life. If you have to go to school or study hard or go through hardships in your life, it is only to create a better future with a greater number and intensity of good experiences during your life.

CHAPTER 81
LIFE WOULD BE VERY DIFFERENT FOR MANY PEOPLE
1/10/2011

Recently, I have become a control freak. I feel and think that everything that happens around me is guided and caused by me and that I can somehow magically control the direction of movement of life.

I make a decision that prices of houses or other commodities like gold should go in a certain direction, and when they don't, I get disappointed. I make a decision that my kids should be doing something in a certain way, and when they don't, I make a poor judgment of them and myself. I make a decision that certain people should act in a certain way towards me or their families, and when they don't, I get dismayed. I make a decision that global companies and other countries should be performing in a certain way, and when they don't, I get disgruntled. I make a decision that I should be treated in a certain way to my benefit by my family, friends, corporations and companies, governing bodies, countries, the universe, and life, and when I don't, I feel worthless and disappointed.

So today, I woke up believing that somehow a magical power was bestowed upon me and that everything that I wanted to control would be controlled by me. Everything that I wanted to happen in a certain way, it would. Everyone that I wanted to behave in a certain way would. I would be making my own movie of my life. I would be the writer, the actor, the director, and the producer of this movie. How would life be very different for many people? I know I am a fair person, and I want equality and righteousness and prosperity and abundance to flow all over the world, and hence, the world would be a better place for everyone. But there is something bigger in the works that I need to become aware of. There is a plan for everything, and everything is meant to come about and happen in a certain way in order to complete my growth. I need to have Faith that what is happening around me is all meant for a good purpose and that my purpose is to make everybody grow to become a better soul, a more complete being.

Suddenly, I realized that even though it seemed that I was not in control of anything, I was in control of one of the most important things: my faith. Yes, I can have faith that everything is for a reason, and it is always a good reason. This control allows me to respond to everything that happens around me in a certain way that allows me to become my best self. Life would be very different for a lot of people if I didn't have this faith. Life is very different for a lot of people because I have this faith.

CHAPTER 82
REAPPEARING ACT
3/4/2011

Have you noticed how things you don't like keep reappearing in your life? That chipped coffee mug that you always replace with a new one and chips the first week it is put into use. Or the light bulbs that keep burning out, and it always is the light bulb that is hardest to get to. Sometimes, it is the type of person you come across in your life, and if you look back, you see you have had this type of person again and again in your life. Take your worries, always worrying about the same thing over and over again. You start worrying about your health, and as soon as you clear that worry with all the medical tests available, you find another little pain or spot on your skin to worry about. I even see it in my practice. A dentist by profession, I like to see people with healthy teeth and gums. But I keep seeing people come with the same problem over and over again. And if there is one kind of cavity filling I hate doing most, it is the one that keeps reappearing the most. The same holds true for my patients. I see there are ones who really try hard to take care of their teeth but come up with the same problem constantly. If someone is scared of breaking teeth, he constantly breaks his teeth. Someone else who is scared of losing teeth because their parents lost their teeth to gum disease will always end up with gum disease. If you get a flat tire and hate having a flat tire, guess what? There is another one on its way.

So what is in the nature of life that makes these kinds of things repeat in our path? Just because our mind is concentrated on it, we notice it more, or because we pay so much attention and notice to it, our power of intention gets tweaked in a way that makes it come back. But if that were true, then I would think that the power of intention would make all the good things that you like to come back to. You love a cup of coffee that is perfect in temperature when delivered to your table at the restaurant; good luck, it seldom happens. Honestly, you just put up with it because you have gotten tired of asking for the right one. So now it makes me think. By virtue of not liking something, do we make it occur in our life over and over again? Is life trying to make a perfect customer out of us; every time it serves as a dish, and we don't like it, it serves it again and again until we show our gratitude and acceptance.

Could it be that if we are presented with things in our life that we don't like, all we have to do is accept it and just say thanks for being here in my life? I know you have a purpose. Then, will it stop from reoccurring and repeating? When the light bulb burns, say thanks. It was a good exercise to replace it because I am learning how to replace light bulbs fast and efficiently. The flower that you keep planting and keeps dying on you don't look at the dying part; look at how it gave you life while it was there. Embrace what appears in your life because maybe that is when it will stop reappearing in the same way. Accept, forgive, and forgo because maybe that is the only way you can prevent undesirable things from happening in your life. When the drainpipe gets clogged and you are pumping it, instead of concentrating on how terrible it is that the pipe gets clogged over and over, look at the moment that it starts flowing again and say, "Ah, this looks so good.

Life continues to present you with events and challenges until you become accepting of them, be okay with them, and not show a blast of energy to them. Let it be and flow away. Only show your blast of energy when you are presented with something you like and want to keep reappearing in your life, your good life.

CHAPTER 83
FAITH
4/9/2011

Recently, I have been asking myself what faith is. Is it good? Where does it come from? What happens that strengthens or demolishes it? Is it necessary or just a luxury?

I don't think anyone has the answers, but I think I got close when I went to the Temple this morning. As I entered during the part of the service when the Torah was being returned to the Arch, I saw this old man trying to stand up from his wheelchair to get close to the railing so that when the Torah was carried nearby, he could stretch his arms and reach it. He was having great difficulty getting up, and the strong helper was trying very hard to lift him, and he still couldn't get up, but yet, as the Torah was getting near, he stood up and bent forward to support his weight on the railing. It was definitely an effort to do what he was doing, yet his faith steered him toward getting the energy to accept the hardship. I think most people would have just said to themselves, "What difference does it make, I'll just waive from my wheelchair as the Torah is being taken around. I know my prayers will be accepted anyway." So, what makes this person go through the pain of standing up to do more? What makes so many devout religious people do certain things at very odd hours of the day, as hard as they may be, just because they have faith?

Some people have faith in God, some in their religion, some in their country, some in their leader, some in a member of their family or a teacher, and some in themselves. But whatever the target of this faith is, it is the power hidden in the faith itself that drives the person. I started to think to myself that it was time to believe in something, and that was how I would gain the strength to push forward in my journey into life.

Chapter 84
The Unhappy Happy Hour
4/14/2011

It is almost becoming a routine. Come home, dress up, get the house errands in order, jump in the car, and go. When you get to the destination, there is a line of cars waiting to find parking. Do your best to park the closest and start to walk. On the way to the hall, you see many of your friends, some whom you just saw the previous Saturday at the party or some whom you have not seen for a long time. Arriving in the hall, you meet a new challenge, quickly entering and finding a place to sit with as little eyes catching yours, especially if you are arriving a bit late. Getting to the empty seat is a whole ordeal by itself. On this particular night, as I was seated, I noticed this old lady eyeing the empty seat next to me. But she had to get past six other comfortably seated ladies in order to get to the empty seat. With little legroom and nobody willing to stand up to let the old lady go through, she had to use her high school acrobatic maneuvers to get to the seat. As she sat down, she asked me who was talking at the podium and why the speaker's microphone volumes were so low. I didn't know who the speaker was either; the presenter was not doing a good job of introducing the speakers. We sit there listening to the stories and memories of the people who have just passed away, sometimes shedding a few drops of tears because their memories remind us of our own past experiences or of what might be in store for the future, and then at a good break in between the speakers, all of a sudden there is a rush of people to get in another line, the line to show respect to the loved ones of the person who had just passed away.

You see, this is the scene at the memorial services that has become almost a routine these days. After work, forget about going to the local bar for a few drinks and changing the mood before you go home. This has become the happy hour of our society. To follow each other into a huge gathering so that we can pay our respects to our beloved friends and relatives and speedily say goodbye so that we can get home in time for dinner. Oh, and sorry, I forgot. Sometimes, this event is followed by a dinner, which means the unhappy happy hour can now turn into the real happy hour because, in a matter of minutes, everybody forgets about who has just passed away and who is still in mourning, and everybody starts to joke around by looking for something to laugh at or someone to tease, especially all the young unwed singles who have given up the hope of meeting someone at the local club's happy hour, in favor of becoming noticed during the unhappy happy hour.

These memorial services have become so commonplace during the week that if one week goes by without its special recognition, just like addicts who cry in the absence of what they crave, they will cry even at home without even attending the unhappy happy hour.

Chapter 85
Wrong choices
4/16/2011

Recently, I have been thinking to myself if I would live my life differently if I were to live it over again. I don't mean that I would make different major choices. I am talking about the little choices now. The ones that often seemed to not matter and be insignificant but have had a major adverse effect on my life with unsuspecting consequences. I call them wrong choices, and boy, do I wish I could live this life over again and make the right choices this time. I guess all this boils down to one thinking of his life as successful or not. Forget about the major destiny-driven choices, like who you marry, when you have children, what career you choose, and what you study in college. I am talking about all those little choices that today make you feel good, or make you have regrets, or if there is any point in having regrets.

So I remember the time that I lingered on whether to buy this thing or that, and the difference was a bit in the cost, and now it seems that the little I saved in a monetary way had a much larger emotional consequence that was not apparent at the time. Then I look back at that day when I made that certain decision, and I truly understand why I made that decision, but I realize that the basis upon which the decision was made was a creation of my thoughts. I wonder whether it was a fabrication and accumulation of the thoughts of the people around me combined with my lack of experience and expertise. This is how I see why so many young people go in the wrong direction in their lives. Instead of looking at what is real, they fantasize about imaginary conditions.

I remember making decisions about going or not going on this trip or that and spending a few hundred dollars more here or there on buying something. Now I see that in the grand scheme of my life how inconsequential those things would have been, and although at that time things were very uncertain for me, prompting me to make errant decisions, had I not cared about my future, I would have made alternative choices that probably would have led to lesser number of regrets. I look at the past and see that an overriding factor for me in making any decision was whether it was better for my future or not. Never was the question about whether it is something I want now or not or whether it would give me joy and satisfaction in the present. I guess that is what they mean by saying live for the moment, live in the present.

The present is all that counts. I see millions of people who have lost their homes because they took the path of instant gratification and jumped into buying houses they could not afford, but the trick that does it for them is that, at least for a certain amount of time, they get the gratification. As parents, we always want to look into the future for our kids, but where there is no life-threatening danger, is it right to harness their wants and desires? Granted, safety and common sense should always be used, and rash decisions are never acceptable, but for things that have no apparent physical risk but only a perceived disharmony with our thoughts, we should not create such havoc that will cause enduring regrettable thoughts.

So, what will be the wrong choice today?

CHAPTER 86
JUST ANOTHER FRIDAY, OR IS IT?
4/22/2011

I was stepping out of my office for lunch. It had been a slow day, and a few patients didn't show up. I was kind of disappointed because I had not met my expectations. I stepped into the elevator, and after descending a few floors, the elevator stopped at the parking level, and my usual parking attendant walked into the elevator. I had sort of formed a friendship with him because he would help me park my car whenever the lot was full, and I had helped him a few times with the things he needed help with.

His head was kind of bent down when he walked in, and he had a somber look on his face. "Are you okay," I asked. His reply made me think that something was going wrong. "I'm okay, but things are not okay," he replied. Upon inquiring as to what had happened, he said he had just heard that his dad was killed by two men in his country. Tears started to gather up in his eyes. He said he couldn't go to visit him for a long time, and now he is gone. I tried to console him, although I knew my efforts were useless. I really felt bad. Only a few minutes earlier, I had been disappointed in life because I was not busy enough in my office, and now, I learned that this guy had just lost his dad, probably for some stupid reason. I felt sorrow, compassion, and frustration, especially since I could not help in any way.

I started to walk in the street, and past the intersection, this very big guy in ragged clothes started to walk right next to me. I felt uneasy at first, but then the guy said hello to me, and I kind of felt okay. I noticed he was carrying a plastic bag full of plastic bottles in it. In my mind, I thought how disadvantaged this guy should be to have to carry these plastic bottles in exchange for some money. Because of what had happened in the elevator with the parking guy, my feeling of sorrow and compassion was highly ignited. I felt I wanted to help him. I turned to him and asked, "How much for the bag with everything in it." He gave me a weird look, kept walking, and mumbled something to the effect of "Are you sure you want to buy this bag?" I became more curious to help the guy out. So, I stopped and turned to him and told him that I was serious and that I was willing to give him $50 for the bag. I figured, at most, he could fetch $5 at the recyclers for the bag, so I thought my offer would be stunningly favorable. I thought I would be making the guy's day by releasing him of the responsibility of walking all the way over to the recyclers just for a few bucks. But his reply stunned me. He said that $50 was not enough. So, I thought maybe he thought that I was teasing him, and he was in no mood to be joked around with. I took a $50 bill that I knew I had in my pocket, offered it to him, and showed him that I was serious about the offer. I kept waving the money at him and telling him to take it and that it was a good exchange. Suddenly, a police car pulled up, and the two cops got out and told us to keep our hands up. I was stunned; I didn't know; I couldn't even imagine what had happened. They walked up to me and told me I was being arrested for attempting to purchase drugs. They said he was a dealer, and they had been following him to find his clientele or distributors. I was shocked. I could see my whole life going past me. This could ruin everything. I didn't know I was buying trouble. I was just trying to help the poor guy. But somehow, now I was tangled in the middle of it all.

In an instant, I snapped out of my bizarre daydreaming. Thankfully, the whole story about me taking the money out of my pocket and offering to buy the bag and the cops was all imaginary! But I was flabbergasted at how my mind was able to see and travel the worst-case scenario when I saw the guy and thought of helping him. I started to wonder whether the bad news that I had heard a few minutes earlier had affected me to the degree that I was thinking unrealistic, bad thoughts. However, at the same time, I thought to myself how easy it is for a benevolent person to be mistaken for a crook and be judged in a way that would turn his life upside down.

There was much to be thankful for as I continued to stroll along the sidewalk. The sun was shining brightly on my back, and I could go back to my office, and no matter how miserable the day was for some, I did not have to be miserable.

Chapter 87
15 Years
5/5/2011

It has been a pretty eventless day. I went to work, did what I had to do, paid the employees, closed the books, and started to drive home. Today, I had to do something I had done 15 years ago again. Many thoughts were rolling through my head. Would I have even thought the same thoughts 15 years ago if I had known everything I know now? I was being rolled into the tunnel. This magical machine would tell me if there was anything unusual going on in my head and neck. A big difference between now and 15 years ago is that back then, I had this cancerous ball in my neck, and I knew something was absolutely wrong, but now there is no physical evidence, and I should feel that things are okay. But I can't help but remember all the events that happened between then and now. It has been a long time since I have grown a lot, but all the same thoughts appear in my head all over again. All the worries and all the speculations become alive in the blink of an eye. What is it about this MRI machine that has so much power? It can determine the path of one's life for years to come. It can change destinies, relationships, moods, abilities, and ideals.

It's funny, but the noises the machine makes have not changed in 15 years. The thoughts in my head while I hear those noises have not changed. The way I shed tears has not changed. The faces of the people who come to my mind have not changed. The instructions of the MRI operator have not changed. The prayers I recant while lying steady on this thin table have not changed. I just hope that the result that this test shows has changed. Hard to know. Hard to expect. Hard to imagine. What if.................?

CHAPTER 88
THE COST OF THINGS
7/5/2011

Life has become so expensive. Everything has a cost related to it; even air is not free anymore. Not only do you get charged for everything nowadays, but you even get charged double, once because of what you want and once because they can charge you double. Try, for example, renting a house. Whatever happened to the days of fair prices? When they know you want the house, the landlord will immediately have another offer for the exact same property, as if there is nothing else available in this big town. And if you are renting a place for business, surely you can pay twice the rent because you will be making money in this location, and if you are making any money, the landlord has the right to the money you make. And oh yes, if you have been living in this space for a year or two, instead of receiving the benefit of peace of mind that the landlord had and the money you saved him, you should get charged for your desire to keep the rental, double charged, just because you have been a good tenant. So, this whole past month, I have been counting and noticing all the different places where I have been forced to overpay for things that I shouldn't have to.

This week, I had to go see a therapist for an issue that I had recently discovered. He suggested that the computer disc of my memory had been corrupted, and so I needed to see him for a good number of sessions in order to erase all the harm and be able to get on with life. My mental computer added up the numbers very quickly. At $200 per hour, one session per week for 8 to 12 weeks, that comes out to a zillion dollars. All of a sudden, everything else that I had to pay for looked so cheap. Car air conditioning for $800. That's nothing; it is only four therapy sessions where I sit and talk for an hour. After four hours of talking in exchange for a cool drive in the summer heat, all of a sudden, the repair job looked so cheap. A weekend getaway at the St Regis Hotel, which is an expensive hotel for $400 a night; why would I go to that hotel? But wait, it is only two therapy sessions. Twenty-four hours of comfort and luxury in exchange for 2 hours of talking. The choice looks obvious. A thousand extra dollars for this month's rent to my wonderful landlord. Who cares? It is only 5 hours on the couch at the therapist's office. Honestly, tell me which one is worth more: a couch or a whole house with bathrooms and carpeting and a kitchen.

So, as I am going through my day, I realize that everything in life is so cheap. Now that I am not going to the therapy sessions every day or at all, I can afford to pay for everything in my life. Even the things that cost double are still cheap because they are being paid for by cheap talk.

CHAPTER 89
THE RAINBOW
7/16/2011

It started to rain a few minutes ago, right when the sun was still shining in the half-blue sky. Suddenly, the brightest rainbow appeared in the sky with all its majestic colors. I am almost certain that everybody has seen a rainbow. It is the most sought-after natural occurrence, and because it is a rare event, just like a shooting star, it makes it so special. I am also sure that you have heard about the pot of gold at the end of the rainbow, and that is the most imagined treasure in the world, too. Never to be found. So, I asked myself why it is that people have not found the pot of gold at the end of the rainbow. All you need is to look up in the sky and locate where the rainbow is, look where the rainbow is touching the ground, pinpoint it, and go there. The pot of gold should be right there.

But of course, there are two problems with that. One is that when you see a rainbow in the sky, by the time you get to where the rainbow is touching the ground, the rain or the sun rays that have created the rainbow are gone, and so the rainbow is gone too, along with the pot of gold at the end of it. But second and most importantly, the rainbow that you see is only there because of you being where you are. If you were somewhere else, that rainbow would not have been where you see it; it would be somewhere else. Therefore, the pot of gold at the end of the rainbow would be somewhere else, too. The rainbow is there only because of you and you being where you are, in the right place at the right time. The pot of gold is where it is at that time for someone else owning it, not you. You were meant to see the rainbow, and someone else was meant to find the treasure. The only way that there could be any winner in this is for you to stay where you are and imagine that someone else is going to be the beneficiary of your vision. Don't even try to find out who the beneficiary of your vision was; just trust that because you were where you were at that point in time, there was a pot of gold for someone to have. That should be reward enough for you.

A rainbow is a great example of real life. You will never find out if it is real or just a figment of your imagination, and the rainbow that you see is only seen by you; another person is seeing their own rainbow, not yours, even though you both may be imagining that you are looking at the same rainbow because even a short distance away from your eye, is receiving a whole different group of rays being reflected by the raindrops that create the rainbow. All of us, even though we are living the same lifetime, are seeing, experiencing, and living different spectrums of lives.

CHAPTER 90
SHOULD DO VERSUS WANT TO DO
7/23/2011

I should wake up by 7 AM, be in my car by 8:30, and arrive at work on time so I don't mess up my work schedule. I should finish my patient's work on time because they have to go to work on time, and I should start my next patient on time because I don't want to hear complaints from them. I should go home, make sure I made enough money to pay for the rent and put food on the table. I should have dinner on time so I don't get an upset stomach when I sleep, and I should go to bed by 11 so I am not drowsy the next day for work.

These are some of the shoulds of my regular work week, and many more exist and many more that I follow every day. But today, all of a sudden, it occurred to me that there is this group of people who live their day not by the shoulds but by the wants. They wake up when they want to, they go to work or school when they want, don't care if they are late, don't have to go home after work, don't have to sleep at a certain time, and don't have boundaries in their lives. And even if they do have boundaries in their lives, they don't have to follow them. Or they don't feel obligated to follow them or don't feel compelled to adhere to them. They simply do things because they want to, when they want to, and how they want to.

I know that some people should and have to do things because it is required of them, and they are expected to because their employer or their government requires it. They are forced to live by the rules; otherwise, there are consequences, but then I see that even amongst those people, many do what they want to do regardless of the possible outcome or consequences. For example, consider how many people should consider safe sex when they are having sex, but they don't, just because they don't want to. Some suffer, but most don't, and most end up having done what they wanted to and feeling happy about it. But is that all?

So, the question that comes to my mind now is that whether "Should" versus "Want" has anything to do with happiness. Am I going to be happier if I have a list of things that I should do and follow the list and, at the end of the day, put checkmarks in front of all the lines, or will I be happier if I follow a general idea of what needs to be done for the week and do it when I want to do it and whatever of it I want to do? This may have huge implications for our society. Imagine if everyone around us did what they wanted to do. It is almost an impossible dream. Nobody would work because everybody would want to have only fun and would want to do only things that were fun. But obviously, that is not what I am talking about. We all have to do a series of things in order to make a living and survive. But then there are so many other things that are made up by our minds only, taking their roots from our worries and fears. We should save for retirement because what will we do if retirement arrives and we don't have any savings? Compared to why should I save for retirement when I can use that money right now to have the things I want to have now? Who knows if retirement will ever arrive, if I will be there, and if I will still want any of the things I want now?

I clearly see two categories of people in my life: those who make their decisions based on what they want to do and those who put priority on what they should do or what is asked of them, so to speak. Honestly, I see a great deal of happiness and contentment with those who do what they want to do because, at the end of the day, both have done what they had to do, but one did it while they engaged willingly, and the other unwillingly. Additionally, I think that there is a higher level of satisfaction with one's soul when you participate in life doing what you want and the way you want, compared to what you should and the way you should. Obviously, a set of rules exists that limit what is right and what is wrong to do, but my argument is that within that limit of common sense and respect for others and other's rights, your soul would be more satisfied when you live your life by what you want to do and not by what you should do.

CHAPTER 91
WAKING UP TO A NEW WORLD
8/12/2011

It's an early Friday morning in August, and although usually in this month, the sun is in full blast by 8 AM, today the haze and the thick low clouds have made everything look grey. No sign of the struggling sun is evident, and the day looks pretty dark. My wife gets up early in the morning to give me a ride to the hospital.

I enter this surgicenter that looks very busy and crowded. Within a few minutes, I am guided into a changing room and instructed to wear this old run-down robe and then go to curtain number 3. I changed, the whole time thinking of the grey clouds outside, and then entered the room and lay down on the bed. I started to think to myself. Crazy thoughts started to navigate my mind. I recalled that the doctor had told me they were going to use propofol, the same medicine that resulted in Michael Jackson's death. I started to wonder to myself. What if I don't wake up? What if these are my last minutes and days here? Have I said goodbye to everybody who cares? Does everybody know where I am, is the day going to change any bit, will it look any different after the show?

Then I thought to myself that as I go into this deep sleep, life elsewhere goes on, and although I will have checked out for an hour or so, so many things in this world will be changed forever. I wondered if this was a means for resetting the clock on my life and path. Am I going to be put back on the right path of progress after having been derailed off course for the past 15 years because of the other event where I was put to sleep? Come to think of it; I have no control over how and when I fall asleep and when I wake up from the anesthesia. Two split seconds in my life are separated by a timeline that can change everything. I gently close my eyes and start to pray. I pray that I wake up to a different world, one that is more congruent with my ideals and lifestyle, one where respect and mutual cooperation overcome self-promotion and trickery. I pray to wake up to a world that is more dependable and just without creating constant hassles, headaches, and unbelievable adverse events. I hope to wake up to a world where life flows like a smooth river, and I am floating on a canoe guiding it to the right riverbank, each time to pick up what I need to move on for my Journey into Life.

CHAPTER 92
I'VE DONE WELL
11/6/2011

Today started kind of crummy. When I woke up, it was raining hard, and even though daylight savings had ended and it was supposed to be bright when I woke up, it was still dark and gloomy at 8 AM. But as the day went by, it started to brighten up, both in the sky and in my life.

After I had my breakfast around 9, I remembered that my son was supposed to come back from his apartment at school so he could join us for going to a fund-raising event in Los Angeles. He hasn't been home in four weeks. I miss him. I thought I better call him so he knows that because of the rain, the roads will be slower. After I had talked to him and his assurance that he would leave early enough to get here in time, I remembered that my daughter had also stayed home last night and had skipped sleeping in her apartment at school. Although she lives closer to home than my son, we don't get to see her often because she is always so busy. I figured since she was home, it was raining, and there wasn't much that could be done; it was a good opportunity to wake her up and spend some time together.

After about two hours, we all got in the car and went to the event. We came across a few celebrities at the event, and it turned out to be fun. When we came back home, my son said he had to go to his room to get ready and leave soon to go back to school. Realizing that I didn't have much time with him, I followed him up there. While he was packing, he started to tell me how glad he was that he was back at home and how much he missed home. He went on to say that even though his place is right by the beach and his bed over there is twice the size of his bed at home, there is something about home that makes him feel good.

Later that evening, my daughter, after having finished some of her studies, packed up and started to leave. I followed her to her car. She turned around and gave me a big hug and a kiss. Then she started to tell me how glad she was that she was only living at school this one year of her four years of college. Her words were telling the tale of being homesick. Although she is a very independent person, I realized that for her, home was also a place of comfort and happiness.

Soon, everybody was gone, and I was alone by myself. But somehow, I didn't feel depressed like other times when the kids had left for school. I realized that I must have done something right during all those years that they were home to make them feel so good about home and love their home and their family. The kids, as grown up and as independent as they have become, they feel connected to their home. I've done good.

CHAPTER 93
CARE
11/20/2011

Do you care? Have I cared? Should we care? Are they caring?

Care is such an important word. I was thinking today about how I have cared to give my patients the best treatment, do the best for my kids, be fair to others, and leave a good name behind. How I care not to make mistakes for my own life and where it concerns others.

But do others care? Does my neighbor care? Does my doctor care? Does my landlord care? Does my friend care? Does my congressman care? Does my mayor care? Does my country care? Does my bank care? Does my boss care?

A mother cares to give her child the best care. But what level of care is considered the best? Is it the best that there is, or is it the best that is possible for that person?

So, I started my day and decided to pay attention to the people I come across to see if I care, or if they care, in the dealings and communications that we had with each other.

I woke up, and it was pouring rain, and my housekeeper had to go to her friend's house. She had cooked some food for them and packed it in a bag, and she was ready to step out when I asked her how she was going to get to her destination. She would have to take two buses, and with the wait time in between, it would take her an hour and a half to get there in the rain. I told her I didn't want her to get wet and cold and I would give her a ride to the second bus. It would be much easier for her that way. We rushed to drive to the bus stop so she wouldn't miss the bus. I cared. On the way there, she tells me to drive back slowly and be careful because of the rain. She cared.

Later, I went to the restaurant to have some breakfast. The waitress asked me if I wanted any coffee. I wasn't sure if she cared or if it was just her job to ask. I got to the office, and the parking guy was roaming around to check for empty spots, and he directed me to one. He was caring and wanted to make it easier for me to park. I walked into my office, and my secretary asked me how my weekend was. Surely, she didn't care. My patient walked in, and she surely cared about being on time. I started to work on time because I cared about giving her the best that I could offer. I was careful the whole time I was working on her. When I was finished, she took care to thank me and my staff for taking care of her needs. I went out to lunch, and there was an old man on the edge of the sidewalk holding a cup out for donations and wishing every passerby a "Good afternoon." I don't think he cared about the people or anyone having a good afternoon. He was too robotic. All he cared was for money to be put in his cup. The pedestrians didn't care about him either. It didn't matter if he was hungry or not. They just didn't care. On the corner, I saw a parking enforcement guy get out of his car, quickly write a ticket in 2 seconds, and place it on the car windshield. He didn't even look around to see if the owner was running to the car or not. It didn't matter. He didn't care. The car was an old car. It looked like the owner barely had enough money to keep the car up, and now he had to pay a $59 fine. The parking enforcer didn't care if that ticket meant the car owner's children would have to skip dinner or much-needed medicine to pay for the ticket. He had a job to do. He cared about the job but not about the person. I was worrying about the person, and I didn't even know him. I cared about the consequences of the parking ticket. But of what good was my caring? It would not protect or benefit anyone. There was no beneficiary in my care. Did it matter that I was caring?

We all too often do things in a robotic manner and then add a word to show that we care. But our actions often come short. We think that others get fooled by our words, and we don't notice that others can easily pick up the message from our body language as to whether we genuinely care or not. Of course, it is an art to be able to master the task of showing and making someone believe that you really care, but is it that difficult or that different to really care? What if the next time that we wanted to make it appear as if we really cared, we would really care from the bottom of our hearts? Make them feel good, but more importantly, make ourselves feel good. Who is actually the beneficiary of our truthful caring?

CHAPTER 94
LAUGHTER
11/26/2011

It's a beautiful, warm, summer-like day in the middle of winter, right in the middle of the Thanksgiving holiday. I decided to go out for a bicycle ride. As I was climbing up the hill, I heard the sound of laughter. The echo of the laughter was energizing, even though I didn't even know where the laughter was coming from and what it was for. As I got closer to the sound, I noticed this very run-down car parked on the side of the street. There were three people in the car, and they were laughing from the bottom of their hearts with every sentence one of them said. I thought to myself, when was the last time I laughed like that, effortlessly and out of control? I presumably have everything in my life, and the people around me and my friends and family are all pretty well off, too, but when was the last time I came across any of us laughing like that? How can I get my hands on this commodity? It is cheap, although it is very scarce, and it is very valuable when it is present, especially when you don't ask for it. The people in the car didn't seem to own or have much of the material things of this world, but they owned the ability to laugh, probably at very simple things.

Deep down, I felt jealous of them. I am constantly trying to improve both myself and my surroundings and the lives of others. But although there may be simple moments of happiness and pleasure, the laughter is missing. But I am missing one key ingredient to life: how to make everyone laugh. Just think of it: when was the last time you made someone laugh out loud? And do you remember the last time someone made you laugh out loud?

Am I of any value to anyone, including myself, if I cannot fill up the air in this globe with laughter?

CHAPTER 95
THE PENALTY KICKS
12/14/2011

It was about ten years ago, the year 2001. I had decided to coach my son's soccer team. He was ten years old, and although he had a great passion for soccer that I had developed in him since I had always challenged him to one-on-one games, he had never developed a great team mentality. So, I thought if I did this, I would both be following my passion and have a great time spending time on the field with him. The season started with our first win. Somehow, I was good at getting the players to do the right thing, and the team came together very well. We reached the championship game after three months of challenges, being the only undefeated team in the region. All eyes were on us. Although the coach of the other team was a highly regarded coach and a favorite, and he had several great players on his team, everybody knew he had his work cut out. The game was tied 2-2 at halftime, and I knew we would always have the upper hand in the second half because I always kept my best formation for the last quarter. In the last ten minutes of the game, we are still tied when the other team gets a breakaway, and it is their best forward against the best player on my team as a defender. As he tried to go past my defender, he tripped over my defender's leg, which was stretched out to stop the ball, and the referee called for a penalty shot. The score is made on us, and we ultimately lose the championship game. But out of pure Luck, we are told that our region has a wild card and gets to send a second team to the area games, being played at a much higher level.

A month later, it was our second game of the day out of the three games we had to play that day. Ten minutes before the game, I pulled my team together and told them I wanted everyone to practice taking penalty shots. So, we spent our entire ten-minute practice time taking penalty shots. Something deep down told me I may need it. Our second game started against a very strong team, but we were leading 2-1, and there were 20 seconds left in the game when suddenly the other team scored, and we were tied. Since there had to be a winner, the game moved to penalty shots. Would we win this? My mind was racing. The five kicks were taken, and amazingly, my prediction had worked in our favor. Having practiced with my team, we ended up winning the game. We won our next game and went to the Section playoffs.

It was our third and last game of the day; a win would send us to the championship game. We were ahead 1-0, and it was the second half of the game. I knew we could hold on to the lead, and although nervous, I was confident. Suddenly, I saw the assistant referee's flag go up and call for a kick right outside the penalty area because, apparently, our keeper had stepped out by inches when he was going for a punt. A totally unfair kick was awarded to the other team, but nonetheless, it was taken and scored, and the game was tied. We did not make it to the championship game. The whole team was crying because they knew it was the end of an amazing season.

Fast forward nine years, and it is the year 2010. I am coaching my nephew's team, and we have reached the championship game again. Tied 0-0 at the end of regulation, we go to penalty kicks. Having had the experience from the earlier years, this time, I had practiced the penalty kicks for a whole week with my team. I thought we had it. The kicks were taken and tied after five kicks, and on the sixth kick, our kicker missed the shot, and we lost the game. Another championship lost to penalty kicks. I was wondering to myself, when we won the penalty kicks nine years back, was it because of what I did with the kids, or was it just plain Luck or destiny? Did I have anything to do with the win back then? I was always so proud of myself for having practiced at the last minute and thought that I had caused our win. So how come it didn't happen this time?

A year went by, and I was coaching my second nephew. We had amazingly made it through the playoff pool games, and it was our quarterfinal game. Could we possibly win this game against the number one team in the bracket? Again, knowing that if the game ended in a tie, it would be decided on penalty kicks, I had my team practice penalty kicks before the match and picked my best shooters. We were down 0-1 at halftime. It was the last 10 minutes of the game, and as usual, I had my best formation on the field. We score and tie, and then score again 2 minutes before the end of the game and get ahead 2-1. It looked like we had the game in the bag, and everybody was so excited. At kickoff, there was less than one minute left. The ball is passed to one of their forwards, and he takes it all the way to the corner flag and takes a wild shot toward our goal. There is no other player there except my goalkeeper and the most dependable player on my team, playing defense. The ball bounces off of the dirt, and my keeper misses the ball; the ball bounces away from my goal, and as my defender goes to clear the ball away, the ball takes a wild bounce off the uneven dirt and hits the hand of my player. Without any hesitation, the referee, who had been making all sorts of bad calls against our team the whole game, decided to call a penalty kick. They scored on the kick, and now being tied, the game goes to penalty kicks. Again, I am in the position of winning or losing based on penalty kicks. How is this all going to end? I think to myself in a puzzled way. Is there a message I am supposed to get from all these penalty kicks? I was pretty confident we had this one since I had practiced exactly how I wanted things to go. Four penalty kicks later, we are tied. Last kick, they make the shot, and now the pressure is on our player to score so we can tie it up. My player, who usually has a great kick, goes up to the ball confidently and takes his best shot. It is a good shot. I see everything in slow motion. It probably is about a tenth of a second between when the ball is kicked and when it reaches the goal. The past ten years of soccer games and penalty kicks went through my mind. One after the other, I saw all my previous players take the shots and my goalkeepers blocking the shots. The ball was traveling in the air, and it looked like a great shot when the goalkeeper reached and blocked it. Again, the game was lost, once to an unfair penalty shot and then to kicks from the penalty mark.

Where is the lesson in all this? Was I wrong to think that I had anything to do with my team's win years ago on penalty shots and going to the Area Championship? Is all of this written, and are we there only to enjoy the process and not care about the result?

CHAPTER 96
POINT OF VIEW
2/9/2012

I was at work the other day, doing cosmetic dental work on one of my patients. As usual, I was working in a sitting position behind the patient. It was her front teeth that had chipped and were crooked that I needed to fix. After I had spent an hour finishing and fine-tuning the work, I decided to move to the side and look at the teeth from another viewpoint. I was amazed at how much I would have missed if I had left the work as it was. Looking from behind, everything had started to look good, but as soon as I had shifted my point of view, all the flaws were evident.

Such is the norm in life also. If you look at your customers from behind the desk all the time, you will miss a lot in terms of what information you can get that will benefit you in giving the best service and how you converse and present your product to your customer. If you are a chef and only work behind the grill and never take the time to change your point of view by going to the tables and seeing how your artwork looks on the table in front of the patrons, you will never be able to present your best. If you are a bank manager and talk to the customers only from behind the glass window, you will never understand how everybody feels and what they want. You will never develop the kind of relationship you need to become a successful business. If you are selling a product and only place yourself in the position of the seller and never shift positions to look at what you are selling and how you are selling it, you will never know what is required to make that special sale for that particular person. You will never understand what the flaws in your presentation are if you only talk from behind the podium and never step in front of the podium and look back to see what your audience is seeing. I realized how important it is to view things and our world from two different points of view and to make an analysis based on that.

I also noticed how two people conversing at the same moment in time about the same exact subject matter could have a very different perspective on the issue at hand. The point of view is different, and if we want to be a good listener, it is sometimes necessary to change how we are listening so that we understand the different ways of looking at the issue at the table in the discussion. This then makes me realize why there is usually no progress in talks among politicians and heads of state, ending their arguments in a deadlock. They lack the ability to step outside their perspective and see something from another perspective. They lack the ability, or even much worse, don't want to change their point of view to see what the path to resolution is. They prefer to remain steadfast in the narrow field of vision and look at the problem at hand from only one direction and one path. A husband and wife who end up in a heated argument never have the ability to see what the problem is from the other person's point of interest.

There is a lesson here, which is to be able to shift your vision and the way you look at things, people, or relationships. Then, you will be able to fit the new information that you gather from the new perspective into your collective train of thought and produce an outcome that will be more complete than it could ever have been.

CHAPTER 97
MISUNDERSTOOD
2/24/2012

I have been going through a period of my life recently that caused great aggravation. You see, it is so easy that when you say something and do something, it is interpreted by another person as something else. One may have the best intentions, but if the receiver is seeing it through a filter of his or her own, it becomes distorted to fit the eye of the beholder. I see so many times that parents communicate to their children and spouses to each other, and all is wasted time because the receiver makes judgments and presumptions of their own rather than look at the truthful facts. A teenager comes home late, and a parent is immediately jolted into thinking that something fishy is going on. Why can't people act with integrity and truthfulness with each other? Why do memories of the past and anger from previous encounters fog our view of events today? Then, when we get angry, we make decisions and say things out of anger that lead to wrong decisions. When you are angry, you are not in the position to make decisions because they often end up being decisions that will bring resentment and failed results. When you make decisions with integrity and honesty, you will make truthful decisions that everybody can live with.

But what do you do when you are misunderstood? Do you try to make the other party understand what the truth is? That would rarely work because the listener would still hear things through the dirty lens. Would you ask someone else to convey the message? That may bring better results because the listener does not put on the same lens to hear the message. Does one send a text or email or print it on a piece of paper and put it under the pillow to be found? I don't think that works either because if you listen to the voice as the letter or text is being read, it is often the voice of the reader and not the voice of the writer, and again, that voice is distorted. It seems there is a no-win situation, bringing more frustration and anger.

The only way out is to just simply acknowledge the way someone has understood you, and then without trying to tell them that they made an error in understanding you in that way, just simply try to clarify what you really meant to say. At this point, your job is done, and you must just leave it up to the listener to perhaps, over a period of time, find the correct message that you were trying to convey.

CHAPTER 98
WINNERS
2/26/2012

I have noticed that some people are always winners. Doesn't matter what they do and, where they are, and where they go; they tend to win in whatever they participate. But is this just our perception, or is it real? For example, if we see someone winning at a poker table, is that person a winner in life too, or even a winner in a volleyball game at the beach? Or is winning a comparative action? For example, Mr. B always wins against Mr. A, but Mr. C always wins from Mr. B, but not necessarily from Mr. A.

I ask this because I have a friend who pretty much wins against me in any event, whether it is a sports activity, a board game, or cards. Actually, there is one game that I wonder if he would win from me, and that is chess, but we have never played chess together. So, I wonder if the winners always appear as winners because they only participate in activities that they know they will be winners in or if they will actually win in an event that they do not have much expertise in. Warren Buffet appears to be a real winner in life, but has he ever participated in a tennis game or basketball match? And Kobe Bryant is a real winner in everybody's eyes, but is he really if you ask him to play poker or backgammon?

Do winners approach you and the game or activity they are getting involved in with such confidence that the only result in it is for them to be winners? Sometimes, I wonder if it is the confidence that they are carrying around with them, the intention they put into anything they attempt to do, or if it is Luck. I can understand where they might have gotten their confidence to carry with them, but Luck is not something you can study or acquire or learn to have. Do they have a stronger ability to put their intentions out there? If you are not carrying confidence, are you out of Luck, or can you actually carry some luck with you to overcome the lack of confidence? How about know-how, talent, and ability? Where and how do these things come into play?

I look at the times that I have been a winner. It definitely had to involve my know-how know-how and ability, but not necessarily my talent. Hard work, more often than not, overcame the lack of talent. Confidence was definitely a big thing. When I had it, even when I lost, I still felt like a winner. As far as the role of Luck goes, I go back to my definition of Luck: getting a good result despite a wrong decision. That is the best kind of a winner because it brings the greatest ecstasy and joy. The others just make you feel content because you say in your thoughts to yourself that you deserved it, and you got it.

CHAPTER 99
WHO GAVE WHAT UP?
4/17/2012

The past week and days have been very stressful for my family and me. We thought everything was set for us, only to suddenly find that the things we thought we had arranged to always be there for us were no longer dependably there.

I was at odds with my life. I had given up many good times to be able to someday have something that I really wanted: a house of some sort. I had made sacrifices and closed my eyes on the pain that many times I would have when I would come home from work and work through my tiredness and my back aches. I would never get sick because I would even go to work through my sickness, and it sure was not fun to have the stomach flu or a cold and go to work, so I had no choice but to not get sick or to get sick on weekends or during holidays, which is what usually happened (I would almost always get sick during the holidays preceding New Years, the longest work holiday of the year). Now, when I was getting close to having what I wanted or thought I would have, the closest person in my life decided to want something else, making it difficult, if not impossible, for me to have what I had given up so much to have.

On a parallel note, my brother is going through a difficult time. There is this business that he has worked on for more than 20 years. He started it from scratch, worked day and night and on weekends, putting thoughts and manpower and hours into it to make it profitable and then grew it into something that was giving him a good return and then slowly, the past few years, it has withered, and last week he was given notice that his contract would not be renewed, which basically meant that he would lose the business and something that he had given up so much to create, was disappearing. So, one day, when we were having breakfast together, he started complaining to me about how much he had given up to make that business happen and how hard he had worked all those years to create a business that was now worth nothing and had nothing in it for him. He was sad because he felt betrayed and taken advantage of for giving up so much for it.

We had both become dependent on the businesses that we had created. Our businesses had allowed us to live a good life on a daily basis and have many things, but now it was just like ashes in the wind. We were dismayed.

It wasn't long before I went to work. After a few hours, one of my brother's workers came to my office for some treatment. My assistant, who has been working for me for twenty-five years, was helping me. My patient had worked for my brother for nearly thirty years. As I was deeply immersed in my work with these two people near me, I recalled what they both looked like when I first met them and when they first started to work for my brother and me. When I looked at them and saw how their hair had grown grayish, their skin had wrinkled, and their teeth had worn out, tears started to fill my eyes. I started to ask myself what my assistant would have done if I suddenly dropped dead or got disabled and stopped working. What will become of her? What will happen to my brother's worker when his business closes down? What will he have left over? The words that my brother said bitterly that morning started ringing in my ears. "What have I given up for my business?" And then I looked at these two people and said to myself, what have they given up? All those hours that my assistant spent on the bus to go between work and home and all those long days my patient worked for my brother. They gave up so much being away from their family to make a living for themselves and live a simple life of survival. I was reminded of the cook who has, with great loyalty, shown up to work every day for the past thirty years and worked behind the hot grill on the hot summer days throughout days and nights. What has he given up? Then I looked at my brother, and I noticed that although we had given up so much, we had a business that had earned us a good deal of backbone and money; we had our own belongings, homes, cars, etc. What did these two people have for what they had given up? They had given up so much, too, and had gained nothing. They would be left with nothing if our businesses closed down, but we would still be left with all that our businesses allowed us to purchase. We had given up so much, but what these people had given up was so vast compared to what we had sacrificed. We had so much to live for, after all, and they would have a sheer nothingness for all they had given up.

Suddenly, it appeared to me that my brother and I had realistically not given up that much after all. We had much to be grateful for.

CHAPTER 100
WHEN WHAT HAS BEEN WORKING NO LONGER WORKS
5/2/2012

Today, I was working on one of my patients. I had to give her an injection to get the lower jaw numb. For the past several years, I have had an awesome success rate with this injection, where statistics show that it is only 80% successful. For me, it has been 100%. But in the past few months, it has been a dismal statistic. Especially today, this was the fourth injection that was not working. I was getting very irritated because it was making me late on my schedule, and I was thinking of myself as a failure. I tried blaming the anesthetic, the drug company, and anything I could get my hands on, but none of it mattered; the injections just didn't want to work.

There is another dental procedure that I have been trying for years when I am doing impressions for crowns, and it has always worked perfectly, but recently, I have been having a lot of problems with that technique and material. Neither the material nor my ability to do the simple procedure has changed, but it is amazing how much the result has changed.

So, what happens when something that has always been working all of a sudden does not work? Could it be that because I am having trouble with some other event or issue in my life, the procedures have stopped working? Or is it because the universe has conspired to make me suffer because it wants to show me that it is still in control, not me?

Have you ever noticed that things start to go wrong in bunches? It must be that the way we see things puts us in a mindset that we can no longer focus on the task at hand, and therefore, our margin of error increases. It must be that when we get angry for some reason or at something, we tend not to pay attention to other events in our life the way we are used to, and therefore, we mismanage our actions. That is why when countries are at war, they keep making wrong decisions and make matters worse instead of improving relations. Maybe that is also why when couples get overwhelmed with children in their lives and a new house and new mortgage, they start to make new bad decisions about each other and then end up in divorce proceedings.

Sometimes, it is necessary that when things start to not work, we step aside, take a break, take a vacation, participate in meditation break, end the cycle of wrongness, and start making sensible and correct decisions for our lives.

CHAPTER 101
A SMILE TO GIVE
6/12/2012

There is this couple that comes to my office every so often. They are a couple, but they are not husband and wife or anything like it. The guy is an old guy with plenty of medical ailments. Today, he was actually brought in a wheelchair because now he can't walk anymore because his knees have given out.

She has had an interesting past, too. I remember when she was having chemotherapy and was so weak that he would accompany her to the office to get her dental treatment done. Then, after her chemotherapy, she ended up with such terrible arthritis in her hips despite her young age that she had to have both hip joints replaced in order to be able to walk. Today, she said that finally, after 18 years of living together and taking care of each other, he was moving up north to live with his family because he was getting to be too much of a burden. So, she had brought him in for his final dental checkup before he would move away. When I was finished working, she came to help me get him back in the wheelchair and start their trek home. I remember from a young age, she used to walk with a limp, and now she was trying so hard to push a wheelchair with this heavy-set man sitting in it. In an instant, I recalled all the hardships that she had gone through. Starting with her reaction to the polio vaccine and the resultant limping, and then her lymphoma, losing her job, the hip surgeries, and the prospect of never getting married or having children of her own.

Yet, as she was pushing her friend's wheelchair, she still had a smile to give. She still had a positive attitude toward her life, the life that was handed to her with a full load of problems, but she was not allowing the problems to overcome her. She still had been brave and caring enough to find someone who was even worse off than herself and, by taking care of him, find a purpose in this life. She appears to me as a true fighter, a true believer, and a Tzadik (a righteous person) or an angel. One who, despite all the natural disasters in her life, still smiles at others, ks at life pleasantly, and does what she can to help the world around her by helping one soul breathe easier.

Too many of us have so many blessings in our lives and don't pay attention to them and have yet to find our purpose in life. This lady, despite all that life has poured over her head, has decided to shake the dust off her back and rise to her calling in life, and all that time with a pleasant smile on her face.

CHAPTER 102
RELATIONSHIP CANCER
7/29/2012

Sometimes, I wonder to myself if it is possible that just the same way that people get cancer and get ill, relationships can get ill also. Not that either of the people in the relationship is ill, but just that the air between them gets cloudy and diseased. If such is the case, and there is such a thing as relationship cancer, then just like cancer treatment, it needs chemotherapy and radiation therapy. Otherwise, the relationship will die. You can take aspirins to cover up the disease, or antibiotics to temporarily slow it down, or try to change its course, but if you don't do the right chemotherapy, you won't get rid of the cancer.

So, I wonder to myself. If a relationship ends up having cancer, is it worth it to make it go through chemotherapy, or should one just let it go to death? Of course, letting it go to death means letting the relationship end. That will have consequences. It will be a road less traveled and a diversion from all the goods that life could have in store for a family. People get married because they want to see their relationship grow, get old with each other, and experience grandchildren in their joint homes. Obviously, this will no longer be possible when two people move apart. Many golden dreams will be shattered, and many experiences will be missed. Although there will be a whole set of new experiences, they will not be congruent with the well-being of the unit that started a new life form when the two individuals got married. The act of marriage is one in which people make a binding agreement to love and behold, in good times and in bad, till death. What happens when some people forget the good and bad parts, and as soon as they experience any of the bad, they give up and go? What happened to the part that says to love and behold? Is it that easy to unlove? Is it that easy to unbehold someone who has helped you bring a child into this world another life?

So then it seems that maybe the relationship chemotherapy is a solution. It is a tough one, though. What medication will be chosen, and which one will be the right one that will produce good results? Will there be enough life and power left in the individual partners to withstand this chemotherapy? Will there be enough belief remaining in the system to make the vows stick? Will there be enough willpower remaining in the spirits of the individuals to carry on with life and the relationship when the chemotherapy is over and so much poisonous medicine has been traded in the space between the individuals? Will both parties understand and agree to this chemotherapy? If one does and the other does not, the same issue and problem will go on.

CHAPTER 103
EXPECTATIONS
8/3/2012

We had gone to a dinner at a cousin's house. At the end of the evening, one of the guests posed a question to the group: "Do you have any expectations?"

People started to come up with answers. "You shouldn't have expectations," one said, "Because when you have expectations, and they are not met, you will be disappointed." Someone else said you have to make your expectations in line with what there is because if you expect too much, you will never be satisfied, whereas someone else said if you don't expect too much, then you will never get anything.

Everybody had a point. It all could be true at one time and not true when it would be applied to another person or time in life. The truth is there is no rule and no truth. What I exclaimed, however, was that there are a few things that we all universally expect. For example, we all expect good health. I don't think there is one person in this whole wide world who truthfully does not expect good health. Even a person who drinks and smokes or has high cholesterol expects good health. And when they don't, for whatever reason, whether Luck or by virtue of their actions, such as living an unhealthful lifestyle, they get disappointed. Additionally, I went on to say that people expect that when they do some work for somebody, they get something in return, such as getting paid. Most people expect to get something for what they do, and the more of it they do, the more of a return they expect, and when they do more and receive less in return, they get disappointed. There are very few altruists in the world who would do something without expecting something in return, whether it is money, recognition, blessings, favors, or even just simple love. Those kinds of people are few and far between, and I cannot speak for those people, although I highly admire them, and many of them have been an inspiration to me. But as a rule, even those who work for a cause and not a personal return want to see their cause succeed because of their work, and if it does not, they get disappointed.

Then, a thought came to my mind. What about the people who expect others to do things for them? It is one thing to have an expectation to have something or to get something, but what about the expectation of someone else doing something for you? Maybe you want them to do that thing over and over again. It is your want and desire; it is your expectation of someone else, not an expectation of yourself. Is that a fair expectation? I can understand if someone wishes to have the expectations they have for themselves met, but is it fair to have an expectation of another person to do something or be somewhere or act in a certain way simply because we expect them to? What about work and getting paid? You expect to do work and get paid for your work. You are expecting someone else to do something. Then shouldn't that same principle apply here, too? You have the right to get paid for your work, but do you have the right to expect others to pay you for it? Okay, I agree, you should get paid for your work, but can you expect who you did the work for to pay you, or is it enough if any entity pays you?

We all have many expectations in our lives, and the more we live and the richer our society gets, the more we expect. We expect to have this and that, and the more we expect, whether tangible or intangible, the more we set ourselves up for disappointment. We should maybe simply desire but without expectation.

CHAPTER 104
ASKING FOR MIRACLES
9/17/2012

My family and I had gone to the temple on this day of celebration. It was the celebration of the birth of earth and humanity. The Rabbi was telling a story about how God gives us the choice to ask for miracles, and he makes them happen as long as the miracle is within reach. So, I started to think of all the miracles that I had in my mind, all of which I thought were within reach. And then I received a surprise. God had a plan for me.

You see, a few weeks ago, I attended a festival and seminar in Colorado that promised transformation and awakening. They had invited a handful of the best speakers, writers, and spiritual leaders from around the globe to this 4-day long event. I attended each event with the zeal to find the answer. The way that I could wake up to my life. To see how I could be present in my life. To find answers to my questions. All the whys and why I'm. Although all the speakers were superbly inspiring, at the end of the event, I had found myself no closer to my spirituality than at the beginning of the series. Although I had learned a lot, I had not felt any transformation. I had reentered my life with the same number of questions and unknowns as before and kept living my life in the same normalcy until today.

The day had started as any other day. Drive to the temple, find parking, walk inside, find seats, and listen. But then, suddenly, in the middle of a prayer, the Rabbi pointed to me and, in an inquisitive manner, told me to go up on the platform and lift the Torah to be returned to the ark. Again, although very proud and honored, I asked myself why me. But as I said, God had a plan for me. I went up, and when I was hinted to, I started to pick up the Torah, when, not realizing that because it was the beginning of the year, all the scroll was wrapped to the left bar, and therefore, all the weight was bearing on my left hand. I gave it a second forceful lift, and my wrist gave up again under the weight. I knew I had to do this, especially with the eyes of the whole congregation on me. So, I asked God for strength and gave it one final effort, and this time, I was able to lift the Torah. Afterward, my daughter helped cover the Torah, and I was signaled by the Rabbi to have a seat with the Torah in my arms for what seemed an eternity. Already, this was a miracle. I had no idea when I woke up this morning that I would be the beneficiary of such a blessing. I had to sit there with the Torah in my arms for the next hour as the service proceeded, and the Rabbi went on with her speech. A million thoughts were rushing through my head at that time, and I could feel my mind and body going through the transformation that I had waited for.

Life works in mysterious ways; it gives you what you want, but it does it when it wants. So, we best stop waiting for the miracle to happen. Knowing that it will happen. But live our life meanwhile.

CHAPTER 105
RESPECT
10/7/2012

It's the last day of summer. Well, not really, because summer ended a week ago. But it has still been warm, like summer, so it doesn't feel like summer is over yet. It is a hot, beautiful day, and I'm sitting by the big blue pool, enjoying the sun and celebrating this extended summer. It is going to start to get cold from tomorrow, so that is why I am calling this the last day of summer because it is the last pool day probably, after this it will be too cold to do anything in the pool, and I'll be doing my other forms of workouts. I had a good day at the beach this morning, playing beach volleyball. I had not gone for a while, and it was nice to be back.

But something is bothering me. Something that has bothered me over and over again and again in my lifetime. You see, I don't seem to be able to gather people's respect towards me. I don't seem to be able to make people believe in me. Somehow, it seems to me that they don't trust my power and ability. What I mean is that when we were playing volleyball this morning, my teammates didn't think of me as a good player, and they thought of me less than all the others on the team, so they didn't pass the ball to me as much, so I don't feel included in the game, so I dose off, and then I don't play my personal best, and then it gives them a reason not to pass to me and the cycle goes on. The same thing happened when I was playing soccer on a soccer team or when I played backgammon or even cards. People don't pick me first to be on their team. As a result, I don't start to think highly of myself, and as a result of that, I don't perform the best I can. I even sometimes sabotage my plays to prove to them that they are correct. I know I can be better, and I know that I have been better, but somehow, and for some reason, when I start to play with people who are better than me, I start to play second best. I don't put my best foot forward. Honestly, it is not that I play any worse than the others on the field. Everybody else messes up and makes mistakes just as much as I do. But somehow, my mistakes stand out to the point that people in their heads label me as the person who can't spike the ball, shoot the ball, defend a goal, or make a basket. I can do all of those things. I know I can, and I have proven to myself that I can do it just as well as anyone else, but somehow, I don't infuse that trust in other people and, more importantly, in myself.

So, I start to wonder what it is that makes people think that way of me. What is it in my personality that makes people think that I am not good enough for them or that I am not the greatest player? I know that I am at least as good as the best player on the field, but I don't show it, and I don't prove it. I portray myself maybe as a person of low self-confidence and not as the manly man who deserves respect and demands respect from everybody. Even when I score big, I don't let myself get all the credit, and I try to praise someone else for the greatness of my accomplishment. Why don't I just portray myself as a winner? Why don't I trust myself to the degree that I can make other people believe in me and count me equal to them? Is it because I make too many mistakes in the course of a game? Is it the look on my face when I am trying to do something? Or is it just the way I portray myself and my personality with the language that I use? Or maybe not speaking loud enough to punctuate in everybody's mind the fact that I am as good as them? What am I afraid of? Is there a fear in me? Fear of not being good enough, and that message gets relayed to other people by having it appear on my forehead?

I think there is something I should change in my language or my facial expressions that portray to other people how good I am. I mean not by depicting myself as an obnoxious, arrogant person, but as someone who has complete trust in himself and as someone who has complete trust that other people have trust in him. And maybe then I will be showing something that will make other people take me for who I am and show myself as a winner. Yes, that is what I want to be: a winner. I want other people to see me as a winner, too. So maybe then I will have the respect that I deserve to have and get, and then I will end up getting the things I should get.

CHAPTER 106
REASON
2/1/2013

After many years of looking and searching and waiting, we finally came across a home that would work for us, and we could afford it, and things would finally fall into place. It is also very ironic how this home came our way. How many other opportunities came our way but didn't work out for one reason or another, and how frustrated we got at times because things were not working out? I remember countless nights when I would pray that I would find a home and I could move my family into it and settle down. It has been more than 11 years. I was almost at the point of giving up hope, just like many times before. Every time we would get to a buying point, either the prices would go up, or the financial crisis would happen, or the banks would stop giving loans and not approving us for a loan, or there would be ten offers for what we wanted to buy, and we would not get a chance. So when this house came up again, I was at a point of hopelessness because, again, in a matter of 2 months, the prices of houses that we were looking for had jumped 30 percent, something unheard of. It was crazy, and I thought to myself that here we go again, and we have missed another window of opportunity to buy our home, and I could not see any other opportunities on the horizon for myself. The dead heat of hopelessness was starting to settle in.

But as I was again totally hopeless, this house came our way, and through some miraculous events, we ended up buying it. But there was a catch to it. Time was short, and the bank couldn't give us the loan in time, so we had to gather up money from here and there to complete the purchase and then follow up with the loan. The prayers to buy a house had now turned into prayers to get this loan. I was under so much pressure. So many unknowns, and the days are going by so fast, and there seems to be no end in sight. I keep praying and having hope. But every Friday, my loan officer calls me and says this and that, and we will have the loan completed in another week or two, and the same story repeats the next Friday. So, just like the kid who has cried wolf many times, I have learned not to trust anything. I had become hopeless. I kept praying and wishing. I kept asking God to help me get this loan. All day long, I would be so upset and uptight. All night long, I would be so sleepless and sweat in my sleep, and I would wake up in the middle of the night in deep thoughts. I would keep praying and wishing that I would get this loan.

As I was so immersed in my own personal selfish desire and wish, one night in the middle of a cold, windy night when I was awakened by the whistle of the wind coming through the cracks of the window, just as soon as I started to pray for getting the loan, I was struck with a huge thought. I am so tense about getting a loan for a house that I already own and have paid for. How trivial this desire is compared to all the other things other people would be hoping for. A mother praying for a cure to her child's cancer, and a child praying for his parents not to leave. A wife hopes that her husband comes back healthy from the war. A couple wondering how they are going to pay for their rent and food for their children. A child is praying for food at dinner time. There are so many more important wishes in this world. How stupid it is for me to worry so much about something this trivial. It is not a life-or-death issue. It is not something permanent. It is only money. The same money that is supposed to bring happiness but instead brings worry and pain. There are so many other things in my life that are right and do not need any prayers. I should count my blessings and not worry so much about the loan.

I am so lucky.

CHAPTER 107
NEWFOUND STRENGTH
2/11/2013

We finally bought a new home. I have been trying to get this home loan for the past two months. It has been an arduous undertaking. Although in the beginning, I must say it seemed very easy and straightforward. I got all the documents ready. They called me and said all the documents were in order and looked good, and they even said they were going to pay me a few thousand dollars to get the loan from them and lock in my rate. Unbelievable. I recalled the time that I had to pay so many points and fees to get a loan. Now, they are paying me to get the loan. I was very happy and even felt lucky.

But then things started to hit a stone wall. One appraiser delayed his report, and because of that, we couldn't fund it in time, so we had to borrow from friends to complete the purchase. I had now started to get tense. The loan agent said two weeks, and we will have the loan. Now I was getting nervous; as it got closer to the end of the two weeks, I had my eyes hooked onto the phone to ring. Two weeks and a day passed, and there was still no news, so now I was more worried. Soon, I found my worries were not without foundation. They had screwed up and decided that now we must do a whole new application. I was told it would be another two weeks, and we should have it. I had no other choice. They say two weeks, and that is still not bad. If I start the process with any other bank, it is going to take at least a whole month. So again, nervously, I endured the next two weeks in agony, albeit, and sure enough, at the end of the two weeks, another call came in that would postpone the closing for another two weeks. The requests they had for documents were absurd. The information they were asking for was so out of line. I could tell they were just trying to kill time and delay. Yet I felt helpless because they were my only hope for getting a loan in 2 weeks. How silly was I, thinking it would just be another two weeks? I didn't want to believe that once somebody does not deliver, they will get used to that habit. I still reluctantly chose to ride the storm with that bank in the hope that in 2 weeks, it would happen. Of course, all this waiting was not with its own perils. It was truly working on my nerves.

Sure enough, another two weeks passed, and a new set of excuses and requests. Now I was really frustrated. But soon, I realized I was frustrated and angry because I felt I had no other choice. I felt trapped. I swung into action and finally did what I should have done a while ago. I applied to another bank. All of a sudden, I found new energy and strength in me. I now felt I could tell and ask for things that I previously was scared of, for the fear that there might be consequences. But now that I had another choice and did not feel trapped, there was a newfound strength, boldness, so to speak, and comfort. The nervousness started to go away. Power replaced it. I realized how important it is for one to create choices for themselves. When you are stuck with only one outlet and choice, you feel trapped and powerless in negotiations. By creating second choices for myself, I became more powerful in my thoughts, attitudes, and behavior. Even though the process may be just as arduous as before, at least I will now feel better. All I could hang onto was hope and faith. A month later, not much time in the big scope of things and reality, but what seemed an eternity, the second bank gave us the loan. Even better terms.

Indeed, I am so lucky; having faith and creating choices do matter.

CHAPTER 108
USUAL WORK
8/1/2013

Today, a bunch of workers poured into our house. They were demolishing and removing the pool plaster so we could replaster our pool. There were eight of them, and they came with thick gloves and masks eye, goggles, and very big drills. I was nervous. Very nervous because they were going to cut into the wall of my indoor pool with very fragile tiles lined up the walls on the side of the pool. Do they know how deep to cut, and do they know what to remove and what not to touch? After an hour of preparation, they started to work. The big, noisy drills and jackhammers were going at it and removing chunks from the walls of the pool. Again, I was very nervous, concerned, and deep in thought because I wasn't sure if they were doing it right or not. But since I didn't know anything about removing plaster, all I could do was watch. After about 3 hours, when they had finished all the digging, they stopped, and in a matter of seconds, all eight of them disassembled their power drills and hammers dis, connected the air pressures with a big puffing sound, and gave each other a high five, a sign of victory. I was still shaking from all the noise and all the vibrations from the drilling and hammering and, of course, from all the nervousness about what was going on.

It was just then, when I watched them high-fiving each other that I noticed how much fun they were having doing this thing. Here I was, sweating all morning long, and these people were so relaxed doing what they were doing. I realized that it is only difficult for the observer and not for the doer. I realized why my patients were so petrified at the sound of the dental drill. For them, it was a very unusual thing to hear and feel the drill, whereas for me, it is a very normal daily thing, and I have all the control and knowledge over it. I am doing my job, and it is usual for me, so I am not scared, and I am zipping along, but for them, it is a very rare occurrence, so they have every right to be terrified, especially if they don't know what I am doing, and if I have not instilled enough confidence in them to make them assured that I know exactly what I am doing and how routine it is for me to do what I am doing and that even though it is a big deal for them, it is not a big deal for me. I realized how important it is for me to assure them that they are in good hands and that despite all the noise and commotion, all is proceeding well and normally.

For me, going through the plaster removal was extraordinary and painful, but for someone else, it is usual work, and they don't worry about their usual work. I should learn not to worry about work that appears unusual to me because it is very usual to the person who is doing it.

CHAPTER 109
FEAR
9/24/2015

I am another year older, and many things in me and about me have changed, except for one thing: having fear.

I don't know when it all started and how it took root in me. I don't remember myself being such as a child, nor even in my teens. Shy, yes, but I was fearless. I would take it upon myself to do any task and climb any rock........Aha, I remember the first time I experienced fear.

My cousin and I were hiking this mountain, traveling up the path that led to the top of this very steep hill. My cousin said this takes too long; let us just take shortcuts, and we will catch the path later on up there. We did, and after about twenty yards, just as soon as I worked my way up over a big bump and hurdle, my foot slipped on the round pebbles that had gathered in that area. I fell and kept sliding, and as I was trying to dig my foot into the ground to stop myself, I noticed that the whole area was covered with loose gravel; there was no stopping it, and I could easily keep sliding until I would roll over this bump, and then, of course, there would be no stopping to that as I would roll down the rest of the way and injure myself badly. I suddenly noticed this small dry branch of a plant sticking out from the ground and grabbed it, and I was able to stop myself from sliding more. I tried to use the branch to hold myself and plant my tip toes in the ground to pick myself up, but I would slip and slide each time. I was giving up. I just didn't want to make any more moves, thinking that I could stay there until help arrived. My cousin was looking at me from afar but couldn't come to help me since I had slid into the loose gravel area. I could really feel fear in me. The heat of the sun on my back was no help either.

Suddenly, this local kid shows up out of nowhere. Bending his knees masterfully to keep a low profile, he works his way towards me. He grabs my free hand as I am lying flat on my stomach and encourages me to make small, slow movements to pick myself up and lean in a way to not slip anymore. I followed his instructions carefully, and I was able to get up and, with his help, walk my way to safety.

So now I remember that as soon as I had experienced vulnerability, I became a different person, and for the rest of my life, I carried this fear of falling and not being able to get up. It had become my barrier to success. It has caused me to become a cautious person in every aspect of my life. Now I see why I am scared to take chances in real estate investments or other deals. Why am I not willing to try to take the shortcuts and leave the path to try a new journey?

So now I think to myself how I can overcome that fear and erase the memory from my head so I can go about creating new memories and experiences for myself, allowing myself a chance to be a winner again. I like to be a winner, so why not let go of the chain that has been keeping me down? Worse than losing it all is the FEAR of losing it all. It appears to have much greater force and be attached to emotions and have more power over my thinking and doing.

So, as I was listening to the Rabbi in the temple during The New Year prayers encouraging us to take one good thing with us to improve ourselves over this year, I thought to myself, how about getting rid of that old fear luggage and give myself a chance to take a giant leap in my life this year. Make this a year that will count. This would be the best birthday gift for me.

Chapter 110
The Big Win
3/3/2016

Lately, a lot of things have been going against my will, my wish, and my desire. I feel it is a failure, or maybe just a big losing streak. Even simple, small stuff seems to turn out against me. When it seems I am on the path to getting or achieving something and winning at something, the unexpected happens, and I lose it. So, I have gotten into the habit of complaining about this. I act angry and keep complaining to everyone that I am tired of losing, and I can't stand it anymore. I've acted hopeless, helpless, and powerless. I had given up motivation and celebration and replaced it with dismay and sorrow. Until today.

You see, I just remembered what was happening to me 20 years ago, at about this time of the year. Unbeknownst to me, there was this aggressive malignant tumor growing in my neck. In a matter of a month, it grew from the size of a golf ball when I noticed it to the size of a tennis ball when it was removed. It was one of those things they couldn't even figure out at first. It was a rare unknown tumor that usually occurs in children. But when they found out what it was, I had to go through hell to save my life. I always resented what I had to go through because, at that time, I wasn't even sure if it was necessary to go on with the chemo and radiation to survive. But one doctor insisted that I must, and so, to please my family and to make sure I had left no stone unturned on my way to survival, I went through with it. I never knew the value of that advice until today.

You see, back then, there were no good statistics on the survival rate for that kind of cancer. Today, out of curiosity, I just did a search to see what the statistics are. A recent study showed the miraculous numbers. The chance of 5-year survival without the presence of metastasis at the time of discovery is 50%. The chance of survival where metastasis exists is 0%. Wow, how is it that a tumor the size of a tennis ball has not metastasized yet? The chance of survival without metastasis in a person over age 26 is 30%; I was 38, bringing my chances even lower. The chance of survival when the tumor is in the bone is higher, but when in muscles or soft tissue, it is lower. Mine was in the side of the neck, right next to my jugular vein that takes blood to the brain, which translates into poor statistics.

So, I guess when and if I look at it from a different angle, all these small losses or setbacks are nothing compared to the Big Win I had. Imagine how different life would have been without me for so many people. How would my two young kids have made it without my being there and my support? We wouldn't have had our house, our family, all the vacations we went on together, all the memories. How different would life have been for my brother, sister, and mother had I not survived?

I never took note of the Big Win until today. That makes me more cognizant of paying more attention to the now and present.

CHAPTER 111
SO, WHAT NOW?
5/22/2016

What do you do when you realize all your dreams have come true?

Today, I came home from work quite depressed because everywhere I go around me, I see growth and success, but when I look at what I have achieved these past twenty-six years, I see a sea of stagnation. But yet I do my work and come home. On my way home, I stopped at the market. I came out with a hundred dollars worth of food and fruits, and it took me 20 minutes with my last client to make that much money; I looked and said to myself how many people it took to plant all that fruit and package all the food and bring it to the store for me to take. I felt really lucky and blessed to have this opportunity in my life.

Then I came home, expecting that I would spend a couple of hours mingling with my wife and kids. When I got home, I realized that I would be the only person at dinner tonight at home, and everybody was involved in some other form of activity. I wouldn't mind this at all normally, but you see, it has been more than a week since any of us has been able to sit next to each other and talk and have fun.

So, as I became lonely, I hopped on my bike and took a ride up the road from my house. A beautiful road because even though it is near everything, it is secluded and lined with beautiful old trees. They had torn down the house across the street from us, and as I pulled my bike out of the garage to go bicycling on that road, I could only notice the green fence around the construction.

I biked up the hill and made a U-turn at the end of the road. As I was bicycling down, I realized why I like this road so much. It is because this exercise activity always ends in a smooth downhill ride in a beautiful setting. I was coming down and gliding through the crisp evening air with the beautiful rays of the sun flowing through the trees, trying to break the green glaze of the leaves with the yellow light of the powerful sun. Suddenly, I noticed our beautiful white house nestled at the end of the road. As you look down the road, you see a road with trees lined up the sides, and as the road ends, you only see our house, and this is a result of all the vegetation and structure being taken down at the construction site. I couldn't resist. I had to go back up and come downhill again to see if the view still looked as good. As I turned, I noticed that as beautiful as the scene is, at any moment, it changes and turns even more unique and beautiful because the angle at which the rays of the sun travel through the trees changes every second.

I had to turn around and go see that view for myself again. It was heavenly and very rewarding to see what I had achieved to get here and not be aware of it. So, I went to near the top; I started my final glide downhill to my house through the fresh air and the tall green trees. I saw a car coming up, and I moved to the side.

Before I knew it, as I was approaching the car, a pothole appeared right in front of me, and I was late to maneuver to avoid it; my wheel locked, and my bike made me go headfirst into a somersault, and I flew right in the air and landed headfirst onto the asphalt and went totally blank.

And so, I have now ended up on this aisle being taken down by several men of good character. I notice now that I have lived and loved my life to the fullest. Every moment has been a lesson to learn and to appreciate what is, and there is a reason for everything that shows up in our lives, and I have completed my Journey into Life now, for now.